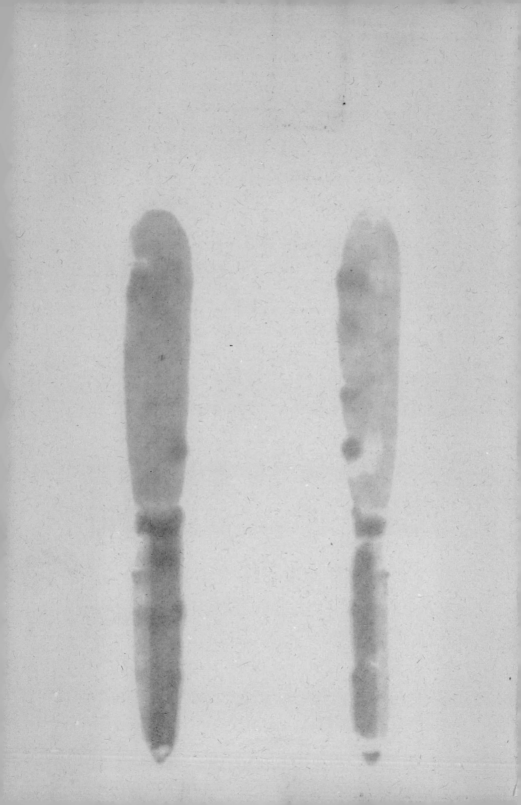

# I Can't Wait Until Tomorrow

### ... 'Cause I Get Better-Looking Every Day

# I Can't Wait Until Tomorrow
## ...'Cause I Get Better-Looking Every Day
# by Joe Willie Namath
### With Dick Schaap

RANDOM HOUSE • NEW YORK

9 8 7 6 5 4

Copyright © 1969 by Random House, Inc.

All rights reserved under International
and Pan-American Copyright Conventions.
Published in the United States by Random House, Inc., New York,
and simultaneously in Canada
by Random House of Canada Limited, Toronto.

Library of Congress Catalog Card Number: 70-89691

Excerpts from "Harper Valley P.T.A.,"
written by Tom T. Hall, are published
and reprinted by permission of Newkeys Music, Inc. Copyright © 1967.

Manufactured in the United States of America
by Haddon Craftsmen, Inc., Scranton, Pennsylvania

Designed by Andrew Roberts

**To My Mother and Father, first;**
to my brothers and my sister; to Frankie C. and
Hugh B. and all my friends, male and female;
and to all my coaches and teammates in high
school, in college and in professional football.
These people helped make this book possible and
helped make my life possible. All of them know
who they are, and all of them know I'm grateful.

# CONTENTS

# I Never Drink
# at Halftime

Howard Cosell, the sportscaster, was standing in front of me on the elevator at the American Broadcasting Company Building in New York. This was several months before Pete Rozelle, the commissioner of football, told me that I wasn't supposed to be seen with undesirables. The elevator was running down, and Howard, as usual, was running on. Most of the time I like Howard. He's a funny guy. He's the kind of guy who, when he meets someone, says very loudly, "This must be a great day for you—meeting me!"

Howard turned to another guy in the crowded elevator and said, in his usual tone, like he's announcing a secret to the whole world, "Did you hear the big news?"

"No," the guy said. "What happened?"

"They found Namath stone-drunk in the gutter this morning," said Cosell. "He got up and he fought the cops. He's suspended from football completely. He's finished."

"What else is new?" said the guy. "Namath's always drunk. He's always stoned. He still thinks he's in high school."

"Is that right?" said Howard.

"Sure," the guy said. "He was a drunk in high school."

Howard grinned. "Well," he said, stepping out from in front of me, "meet Joe Namath."

The guy looked at me sheepishly with kind of a half-smile. "Hi, Joe," he said.

"Man," I said, "get out of here. Get away from me."

This is the sort of thing that happens to me all the time. Here's a guy I don't know, I never even met, and he's saying in front of a whole bunch of people that I was a drunk in high school. Hell, I hardly ever drank in high school, except maybe some red wine once in a while. And I didn't drink much in college, either. I didn't learn how to drink, really, until I got to New York.

I hate all the untrue stories about me. I've always hated getting into trouble for things I didn't do. Guys are always coming up to me and asking me if I know so-and-so. I never heard of the girl, but somebody's told the guy I've been going out with her, and it's his girl, and he's hot. I don't blame him for being hot, but I don't even know the girl. I don't know why people make up stories like that. I could get hurt.

There are always items in the columns about me and various girls, and most of the time I've never met the girls,

4

or at least I haven't seen them in a few years. There must've been dozens of items about me and Kaye Stevens, the singer, about her giving me gifts and us going out on dates and even us getting engaged, and it was all happening in somebody's imagination. I mean, I guess Miss Stevens is a very nice lady—I used to like to listen to her records when I was a kid—but I don't know where anybody got the idea we were going out together. I don't think Miss Stevens would spread stories like that.

There are enough true stories about me without people going around making things up. To hear some of those people, I'm always falling down drunk, and I've had more stewardesses than all the pilots and co-pilots in the country put together. That's crazy. I can't remember the last time I really was drunk, drunk enough to not know what I was doing, and, shoot, there are some airlines I haven't even flown yet.

Hell, I'll admit I've had a drink or two, and I've met some girls, and I've played a few football games in my life. I don't mind talking about the truth. I don't mind telling you about the things that really happened. All I ask is that, when you start reading this book, you try to forget almost everything you've read about me before. Not that there's anything wrong with what's been written about me. It's fine, if you like fiction.

For instance, according to one story I read, Jim Hudson, my roommate on the New York Jets, and I got fined for drinking J. & B. Scotch in Jimmy Fazio's restaurant in Fort Lauderdale after curfew a week before the 1969 Super Bowl game. That story's a lie from top to bottom. In the first place, I drink Johnnie Walker Red, and Jimmy Fazio's not going to run out of Johnnie Walker Red, because he hasn't yet. And Hudson and I didn't get fined. And we weren't out after curfew. Goldang (I always say, "Goldang"; I never take the Lord's name in vain) there wasn't even any curfew that night.

I did get fined once, right before the Super Bowl, and that was $50 for missing a picture session the Monday before the game. Well, hell, the picture session was at ten o'clock in the morning, and we weren't practicing that day. I'm a physical fitness nut, and I believe in getting a good night's sleep every night the week before a game. I'm not going to get up at nine thirty or something and ruin my night's sleep. I've got to get my five or six hours every single night.

Now, take that big story that came out of the Super Bowl about the argument that Lou Michaels, the place-kicker for the Colts, and I supposedly had. All the stories said that we almost came to blows. None of the stories, as far as I know, mentioned the fact that Lou Michaels and my brother Frank roomed together at the University of Kentucky, and that I met Lou years ago when I was a sophomore at the University of Alabama and he was with the Pittsburgh Steelers. We met in Miami that time, too. I was there to play in the Orange Bowl game, and Lou was there to play in the National Football League runner-up game. Not long after that, Lou visited my brother in Beaver Falls, my hometown, which is just about twenty-eight miles outside Pittsburgh.

When we had our big confrontation before the Super

6

Bowl, we were in Jimmy Fazio's and, of course, I was sipping Johnnie Walker Red. I was standing at the bar with Jim Hudson, and Lou walked over to us, and I greeted him. "Lou," I said, "it's great to see you." And I meant it. Hell, it was an old friendship thing.

We started talking—he asked me how my brother was doing in the insurance business—and, naturally, we got to the game. "Joe," Lou said, "we're gonna kill you."

Lou was kind of smiling, but that was all I needed, and I had to start giving it back. I enjoy that kind of game. I've been a target for some pretty good needlers, guys like Don Rickles, Jack E. Leonard and Jackie Gleason. I was on a show a few years ago with Jack E., and he said, "Joe's a pretty smart boy, bright kid, good kid"—he was really being nice to me—"spent four years in high school at the University of Alabama." He got me; I had no comeback at all, but now I'm getting a little quicker. Early in 1969, just before I played a charity golf match against Gleason in Miami, Jackie and I went on TV with Arnold Palmer, and Jackie made some crack about losing a ball in my beard. Palmer looked at me, and I said, "Jackie's consistent, he's got a fat mouth and a fat belly." It wasn't the funniest line ever, but it was better than nothing—and it may have thrown Gleason off his game. I beat him by three holes in a nine-hole match.

"You don't have a chance, man," I told Lou Michaels.

"We'll beat you by thirty points," Lou said.

"Lou, you're drinking too much," I said. "You really got to be crazy. You're not even gonna win the game. Like, you're gonna get your asses beat."

7

We argued back and forth a bit, all good-natured needling—well, most of it good-natured needling—and Hudson and I sat down at Lou's table, and finally Lou said, "I'll tell you why we're gonna win. I'll tell you why I'm so confident. We got the man lying in the grass."

"Who you mean?" I said. "You mean Johnny?"

"Yeah," Lou said. He meant Johnny U, Johnny Unitas, who used to be my hero; I wore his number, 19, in high school.

"Well, I agree he's been great," I said, "but, goldang, he can't throw across the street. Who you bullshitting?"

"You wait and see what happens," Lou said.

"Yeah, I'll wait and see, man," I said, and then I got a little personal. "But how the hell do you know, Lou?" I said. "Shit, you're a place-kicker. You don't even play any more, you old sonovabitch."

Lou began to get a little hot, so I poured it on him. "Why you sonovabitch," I said, "you ain't even got a chance."

Lou gave me a hard look. "Don't you cuss me, Joe," he said.

Hell, we'd both been cussing for the last half hour.

"Don't you cuss me," he repeated. "Don't you call me names. You want to take it outside?"

Lou was starting to get a little serious, so I had to laugh. I'm not going outside with any 250-pound lineman, even if he is an old man of thirty-two. I'm not going outside with the water boy, not in my condition. Make love, not war, I always say.

Lou loosened up and cooled off and started laughing, too, and he and Dan Sullivan, one of his teammates, and Hudson and I all had one or two or maybe three drinks

**8**

and we all left together. There never was any chance of us getting into a fight. Maybe Lou was going to get into a fight. But not me.

We were both smart enough to realize that we were just jiving. Lou'd been around football too long to think that they were really going to beat us by thirty points; I knew he wasn't serious. And I'd been around football too long to think that the Colts really had no chance against us; he knew I wasn't serious. Of course the Colts had a chance against us. Not much of a chance, but a chance.

I don't know why some people keep misunderstanding me. I don't ever lie. Well, I hardly ever lie. At least, I don't lie to guys. I do either one of two things. I tell the plain truth, like when I said there were five or six quarterbacks in the American Football League better than Baltimore's Earl Morrall—just a simple statement of fact—or I kid a little. When somebody asks me why we lost a game and I say, " 'Cause we were out drinking all night," he ought to realize I'm just saying that, I don't mean it. I take football too seriously to stay out drinking the *whole* night before a game.

But some people seem to hear only what they want to hear. When I'm telling the truth, they think I'm kidding, and when I'm kidding, they think I'm telling the truth. I guess those people are going to have trouble with this book, because a lot of it's going to be serious, and a lot of it's going to be fun, and all of it's going to be me.

I know that some people are going to misunderstand the book and misunderstand me, because that's the way they are. I've got a teammate a lot of people don't understand. I mean Johnny Sample. I've heard people say Johnny's a

**9**

hothead and he's a loudmouth and he's a showboat, and those people don't know what the hell they're talking about. Johnny talks. Johnny says what he believes. He lets you know what's on his mind. He's entitled to. He plays his position so good. That man doesn't smoke. He's never had a drink in his life except maybe half a glass of champagne that night after we won the Super Bowl, and he keeps himself in great shape during the season. His one goal is to win, and I respect him for that, and his teammates respect him—and showed their respect by electing him captain of the defensive team in 1968—and we don't care what anyone else says about Johnny. We know the truth about him.

All I want is for people to know the truth about me and for writers to write the truth about me. I don't care what they say, as long as it's truthful. Take a story that a fellow named Jimmy Breslin wrote about me. I like Jimmy. He walked around the golf course with me one day all hunched over, because he said he'd never been around a golf course before without carrying two bags on his back. I just think about him and I laugh. We did a lot of talking over a lot of Scotch.

But he wrote a story about me, and he said that the night before we played Oakland for the American Football League title on December 29, 1968, I went over to the Summit Hotel with a broad and a bottle and, while the Oakland Raiders were sleeping, I was doing what's right, and then the next morning, while the Oakland Raiders were walking around in their team blazers, I was out on the street wearing my $5,000 fur coat.

That story is just plain ridiculous.

I never wore that fur coat in public.

**10**

# 1

# The
# Harper Valley P.T.A.

> . . . And then you have the nerve to tell me,
> You think that as a mother I'm not fit;
> Well, this is just a little Peyton Place,
> And you're all Harper Valley hypocrites . . .*

I'm a known gambler, and I don't just mean on third down. Anyone who's ever seen me in Las Vegas knows I'm a gambler. I don't go out there to look at the sand. My last three trips to Vegas, I've lost $2,500, $2,500 and $5,000 in the casinos, a total of $10,000, not really much for a gambler. But I do a helluva lot better on third down.

I'm friendly with known gamblers, too. Like, I'm friendly with my mother. When I was a kid, she and a few other ladies in our neighborhood used to send me to a nice man with a quarter and a little slip of paper from each of them. The slip of paper had three digits written on it. I didn't know it at the time, but the ladies were playing the numbers. Later on, when I had a few quarters

* "Harper Valley P.T.A.," by Tom T. Hall.

**13**

of my own, I played the numbers, too. I've been gambling ever since.

I gamble out in the open. I do everything out in the open. I've got a lot of faults, just like almost everyone else I've met, but I'm not a hypocrite. I don't hide things. I hate hypocrisy more than anything else in the world. I hate to see any athlete sounding off about virtue and training and clean living when, the night before, I was out with him, drinking and chasing and having a good time. I don't know how he can look at himself in the mirror.

I don't go to church hardly at all any more, and it's because I don't want to be hypocritical. Actually, I miss church; I wish I could bring myself to go more often. I know I ought to go. I was raised in a pretty religious Roman Catholic atmosphere and I believe in God and I pray almost every night. Most of my prayers are just saying thanks for everything I've got.

But I stopped going to church a few years ago when a priest told me that I had to confess each time I'd been with a woman.

"Why?" I said.

"Because it's a sin," he said.

I don't think that's wrong. I really don't. I think if it's a beautiful thing and it makes two people happy, it's not wrong. Of course, the priest didn't agree with me at all. So I stopped going to church. I wasn't going to go to confession and lie, and I wasn't going to confess something I didn't feel was a sin. I wasn't going to be a hypocrite.

. . .

I didn't know what hypocrisy was until I got into the fight over my part ownership of Bachelors III, a restaurant in New York City. Pete Rozelle, the commissioner of football, told me in June 1969 that if I didn't give up my share of Bachelors III, I'd be suspended from football. I'd be suspended, he said, because, through my ownership of the restaurant, I was associating with undesirable people. By undesirable people, he meant known gamblers. Rozelle said that my association with these people could be damaging to professional football.

My immediate reaction was to refuse to give up my interest in Bachelors III. Instead, I announced that I was retiring from football for one simple, basic reason: I hadn't done anything wrong. I hadn't bet with bookmakers on football games one way or the other. I'd never lost a game on purpose or tried to shave points. I admit I had deliberately given information to gamblers to affect their bets: Before the 1969 Super Bowl, I'd guaranteed that we'd win the game and I'd told everybody—out in the open—to bet on the New York Jets. If that's illegal, I should have been suspended before the Super Bowl game, because everything I said was reported, accurately for a change, in the newspapers.

The whole situation was filled with hypocrisy. I was being told to give up a restaurant because known gamblers came in there, yet the commissioner of football, Pete Rozelle, had negotiated with the Hughes Sports Network, which is owned by Howard Hughes, who also owns four or five gambling casinos in Las Vegas, and Phil Iselin, the president of the New York Jets, was also the president

**15**

of Monmouth Park, the race track, where people go to bet. I didn't feel there was anything wrong with the commissioner negotiating with the Hughes Sports Network, and I didn't feel there was anything wrong with the president of the Jets being president of a race track, and I didn't feel there was anything wrong with me owning a legitimate business. As long as I did my job properly on the football field, why couldn't I own a restaurant?

I was supposed to be different, because I play quarterback, because I throw passes, because my performance in a football game can determine whether my team wins or loses. Why didn't Rozelle or anyone else come out in the open and say what they were thinking: "Hey, Joe, we're afraid that people will suspect you fixed football games." That's what they were thinking, but that wasn't what they said. That isn't a nice thing to say out loud. It isn't even a nice thing to think. If I thought so little of a guy I didn't trust him to put out his best for me every time, hell, I wouldn't try to sell tickets on his name and I wouldn't make promotional films about him. Professional football doesn't have double standards; it's got about ten different standards.

The press was beautiful. The press was really beautiful. "Be a man, Joe," they said. "Sell out." I hadn't done anything wrong, but the newspapermen said I should sell out. They said that for the good of the game I had to be above suspicion. You give some of those guys a free cocktail party—hell, just a free cocktail—and they'll print any side of any story you want to give them, and they were telling me I had to be above suspicion. Then they all rushed over

**16**

to Toots Shor's and patted each other on the back and said that Namath shouldn't have any connection with any restaurant that attracts gamblers.

And then those newspapermen who wrote day after day that I was in the wrong, who cut me up and told me how to put myself together again, were hurt because I didn't sit down with them and tell them everything—tell them my side of the story.

In March of 1969, when I was first shown the list of names of so-called undesirables with whom I was supposed to be associating, I took one look at the list and I said, "Hell, just give me the antipasto and the scampi and a bottle of Bardolino." I mean, I thought it was a menu. I didn't recognize a single name on the list. Well, I didn't recognize many of the names on the list. Later on, when I saw some pictures and heard some first names and some nicknames, then I knew I had at least met most of the people. Sure, they'd been in Bachelors III, and they'd said hello to me, and I'd said hello right back to them.

But I'll tell you, if some of those stories I've read about some of those guys are true, if I ever see any of them again, just by coincidence, and they say hello to me, I'm not going to say hello to them. Hell, no. I'm going to say, "Hello, *sir*." I'm not going to do anything to get those guys upset.

For a few months after I first saw the list, nothing much happened. I heard stories that the New York district attorney's office was looking into Bachelors III, and Bobby Van, one of the managers of the place, talked to people

**17**

in the D. A.'s office and asked for help in keeping undesirables out. You need help. You don't just walk up to these people and say, "Would you please get out of here?" You don't talk like that to sensitive people, and these people, I'm told, are very sensitive, and also excitable.

On the night of June 3, a Tuesday, I went to the New York football writers' banquet, and before the ceremonies began, Weeb Ewbank, the head coach of the New York Jets, called me aside for a little private talk, just him and me and Phil Iselin, the club president, and Jack Danahy, the chief investigator for professional football, and some other guy whose name I don't remember. Danahy did most of the talking. He said that bad things had been going on at Bachelors III, bookmaking and stuff like that, and that someone—he never did say exactly who—was going to raid the place and shut it down the next day. Danahy said that for my own good and the good of football I should sell my half of the club—and sell it by the following day. I was stunned, absolutely shocked.

Then the banquet began, and Bob Vogel, who plays tackle for the Baltimore Colts, got up and delivered the invocation. He kept saying we should all pray for humility. It just wasn't my night.

After the dinner, Pete Rozelle talked to me privately and told me that I didn't have to worry about a raid on the club the next day—his sources were right on that— but that I should meet with him in his office. The following afternoon, Mike Bite and Jimmy Walsh, my attorneys, and I sat down with Rozelle and two of his investigators, Danahy and a guy named Bernie Jackson. Rozelle and I

**18**

respect each other; he thinks I'm a helluva passer and I think he's the best commissioner in pro football. I'm not so wild about Danahy; I've heard stories that, before this situation got out in the open, he told a couple of my team-mates, "I'm going to get that punk"—meaning me. That wasn't very friendly of him.

Rozelle told me and my lawyers that, according to in-formation he'd received, known gamblers had been fre-quenting Bachelors III, the phones in the club had been used by bookmakers and law enforcement agencies were going to close down the place any moment. Rozelle said that, under the terms of the standard pro football contract, players "must not associate with gamblers or other noto-rious characters." He explained that he had the power to discipline anyone who violated the rule. The commissioner told me that I hadn't done anything illegal, but that he felt I had violated the rule, through my connection with Bachelors III, and he had to discipline me. He said that if I didn't sell my half of Bachelors III by Friday—two days later—he would suspend me from professional football.

My lawyers pointed out that I couldn't possibly sell my half of Bachelors III in two days, that because the State Liquor Authority had to approve any transaction, the process had to take a lot longer. Rozelle said I had to at least take the first step toward selling the club; then, when the place got raided, he could say that I had been warned and that I had been shocked, like a good boy, and that I had heeded the warning. He was just worried about ap-pearances.

I felt like I was swimming in hypocrisy. Take that

**19**

standard pro football contract. It doesn't only say that players can't associate with gamblers. It's got a bunch of stupid, meaningless clauses, like one about always wearing ties in hotel lobbies. It also says that players can't drink any intoxicating beverages at any time. If that rule were enforced, each team would have to play with three men, and I don't know what they'd do for owners and coaches.

I didn't tell Rozelle whether I'd sell or not in that first meeting, but when I got out of his office, I was pretty damn angry. I knew I hadn't done anything wrong, but I was being told I had to act like I'd done something wrong. Well, I wasn't going to take that. I wasn't going to sell my half of the club. I felt I had as much right as anyone else in the world to own part of a restaurant.

I'd been involved in Bachelors III for less than a year. Ray Abruzzese, who shares an apartment with me in New York, and I had bought the place—it used to be The Margin Call—because we wanted a club where we could go and where our friends could go and have a good time. We'd hired two managers who really knew the restaurant business, Bobby Van and Joe Dellapina, and they'd helped us make the place a success. Ray, Bobby and I were the Bachelors III; Joe was Husband I, the world's youngest grandfather.

I had fun at Bachelors III. I got a kick out of the people who came to the club. I seem to attract all types, gamblers and judges, socialites and secretaries. I don't work at that; it just happens. I really liked the place, and I couldn't understand why I had to give it up just because I was a professional football player.

**20**

Where was I supposed to go instead—to Toots Shor's? Hell, I'd been in there, and Toots Shor had deliberately spilled a drink on Mike Bite, my lawyer. That was Shor's idea of great humor. His other idea of great humor was for him to call himself and his pals slobs. I wouldn't argue with the man.

All day Thursday, my friends and I discussed Rozelle's ultimatum—and the hypocrisy of professional football. We all felt that, on principle, I should stand up to Rozelle and refuse to sell my share of Bachelors III. Mike Bite and Jimmy Walsh backed me in principle 110 percent, but, as my lawyers and business advisers, they had to point out that if I didn't sell, if I gave up football, I stood to lose as much as $5 million—from my Jet contract, which still had two seasons to run, from endorsements and from various commercial possibilities. From a purely financial point of view, Mike and Jimmy said I ought to sell. Ray Abruzzese knew that business at Bachelors III probably would fall off if I sold out, but he said, "Go ahead, Joe. Sell, man. It's the only smart thing to do." Ray wasn't worrying about himself; he was only worrying about me.

Hell, I knew that selling my share of Bachelors III was the easy way out, the smart solution. But I also knew that if I sold, I'd be wrong. I'd be giving in to Rozelle's theory of guilt by association. I'd be surrendering some of my basic rights just so that I could play football and make money.

There was only one good argument for selling—my position as chairman of the board of Broadway Joe's, a

**21**

nationwide franchising operation that had gone public just a few months earlier. A lot of people had invested in the company, and if I didn't play football, the stock would probably be hurt and a lot of people would be hurt, people who hadn't done anything wrong, who didn't deserve to be hurt. I didn't want to see those people hurt. Very reluctantly, without any enthusiasm, I agreed to sell Bachelors III. Early Thursday evening, Mike Bite phoned Rozelle and told the commissioner that by Friday morning he would draw up papers of sale, the first step toward giving up my half of Bachelors III.

Mike felt pretty good about the decision; he thought I was making the practical move. The commissioner felt pretty good; he had found a solution to a difficult situation. But I didn't feel too good; I felt I was violating my own principles.

Thursday night, one of my Jet teammates, Gerry Philbin, was having the grand opening of his new restaurant out on Long Island, and I'd promised to attend. On the way out, I sat in a rented limousine with Tom Marshall, the president of Broadway Joe's and the man who'd thought up the company. I was still worrying about my decision, still second-guessing myself. "Don't worry about the effect on the stock," Tom Marshall told me. "That's not a factor. You just do what you feel is right."

I knew that selling out wasn't right. By the time we got to Philbin's restaurant, I'd reversed my field. I wasn't going to sell. Instead, as I told several of my teammates, I was going to quit football.

I didn't want to quit football. I didn't want to give up

**22**

the game. I love to play football, but I couldn't see sur-
rending my principles just to play football. Most of my
teammates seemed to agree with me. I had a few glasses
of wine to celebrate the opening, and I kept looking around
the restaurant to see if Philbin was being bothered by undesirables. I didn't spot any sportswriters.

By midnight, I'd spread the word among my friends that
I wasn't giving in to Rozelle's ultimatum, that I was going
to retire from football. We decided that I'd hold a press
conference the next morning to announce my plans. We
decided the conference would be at nine thirty, a ridiculous
hour, in the proper place, Bachelors III.

"Yeah," said Tad Dowd, who's both my friend and a
publicity man for my businesses. "Yeah. We need some
breakfast business for Bachelors."

I had a long, long night, and I didn't get to sleep until
about six or seven in the morning, at least two hours after
my normal bedtime. I woke up around nine o'clock. There
was a lot of noise in my living room. There must have been
eight or ten people there, and most of them were talking.
Mike Bite was arguing with Tad Dowd; Mike obviously
wasn't too pleased by my change in plans. Ray Abruzzese
was his usual self, cheerful, carefree. "The press conference?" I heard Ray telling somebody. "Yeah. It's at
nine thirty. Yeah. If Joe wakes up."

I got up, slipped into a pair of brown-and-white-striped
bells, put on the same blue shirt I'd worn under a tuxedo
to the football dinner a few days earlier, then covered it
this time with a blue windbreaker. When I walked into the
living room, I had to laugh. I mean, outside of Ray, every-

**23**

one looked so damn serious. "What's happening?" I said.

Just as I was getting ready to leave, the phone rang. I actually would have been on time for the nine-thirty press conference—well, I would have been close—if the phone hadn't rung. "It's a Paul Bryant from Alabama," somebody said. "It's the man," said Mike Bite, who knew how much respect I had for Coach Bryant, my college coach. He had heard that I was about to announce my retirement, and he wanted to make sure that I had thought it over carefully, that I realized what I was doing.

"I got to do it, Coach," I said. "It's the right thing."

Coach Bryant and I must have talked for about fifteen or twenty minutes. I knew it was going to hurt him if I didn't play.

Bob Skaff, one of my friends, had ordered a limousine—I was at least going out in style—and after I picked up a container of coffee, we took off for Bachelors III. Along the way, my friends and I discussed what I was going to say. We thought about putting part of the blame for my retirement on my bad knees—under the terms of my contract with the Jets, if I had to quit football because of my knees, I'd still get paid—but I decided to stick entirely to the principle. "Why don't you have a tear or two trickle down your cheek? somebody suggested.

"I'll have enough trouble keeping them back," I said.

When we reached Bachelors III at ten o'clock, I couldn't believe the crowd. I don't think that many sportswriters and sports announcers had ever been awake at that hour in the morning. I was really impressed. They weren't even getting a free meal.

24

I made my way to the back of the restaurant and sat down at a table between Frank Gifford and Kyle Rote, football players turned broadcasters. Then, surrounded by a dozen microphones, I made my announcement. I told about the ultimatum from Rozelle. "I'm not selling," I said. "I quit." I felt the tears rising in my eyes. I guess I didn't realize until that moment exactly how much I would miss football. "They said I'm innocent, but I have to sell," I said. "I can't go along with that. It's principle."

I told everyone that I hadn't done anything wrong, that I was being found guilty by association just because I knew some people who gambled. "My father gambles," I said. "Is there anybody in this room who's ever placed a bet?" One television cameraman raised his hand. "Damn right, Joe," he said. Everybody else in the room was either lazy or lying.

The scene was pretty emotional, I guess, and there were a couple of moments when I thought Rote and Gifford might cry, too. They looked so pained. Howard Cosell was sitting on the far side of Rote, and I know damn well that if Rote and Gifford had cried, Howard would have, too. He doesn't let anybody top him.

After the press conference, I jumped into the limousine and went to the Green Kitchen, a restaurant near my apartment, so that my friends could get some breakfast. I just had a glass of water. Jim Hudson, my roommate on the Jets, and George Sauer, one of my receivers, came to the Green Kitchen, and both of them told reporters that if I didn't play, they wouldn't play either in 1969. Later on, Pete Lammons, another receiver, said the same thing.

**25**

I appreciated their support, but I wasn't trying to drag anybody else with me. Hell, I wanted them to play. I wanted to have somebody to root for.

While we were in the Green Kitchen, a little girl, maybe eight or nine years old, came up to me and asked for my autograph. I gave it to her quick, before she changed her mind. Then her little brother asked for my autograph. "Don't believe everything you read," I told him. He was about four or five years old.

At noon, I rode out to the airport to pick up my girl friend, Suzie Storm, who was flying in from her home in Pensacola, Florida, She had heard what had happened. "Will you still like me if I'm not a football player?" I asked her. I knew the answer, or I never would have asked the question, and Suzie smiled and nodded and held my hand, and I felt a little better. In the car going back to Manhattan, we heard a tape of the press conference, and when it got to the point where I said, "I quit," and my voice started to break, I told the chauffeur to switch to some music. I didn't want to hear any more.

All afternoon and into the evening, my phone rang, friends calling to tell me that they were behind me. Marty Schottenheimer, an old friend who plays linebacker for Buffalo, called first; then Johnny Hadl, the quarterback, called for San Diego; then my teammates, Winston Hill and Bob Talamini. My brothers called me, and so did my mother and my father. Neither my mother nor my father seemed upset by my decision; they both wanted me to do whatever I felt was right, and both of them had always worried about my legs' getting hurt playing football.

**26**

By the evening, I hadn't talked to my coach—Weeb had called when I was catching up on my sleep—but he had talked to the press. "This is what I have to put up with," he told one reporter. Weeb has a real knack for saying the right thing at the right time.

The sports experts were already beginning to offer free advice, and some of them were saying I had to sell because I owed the game of football too much not to play. That's bullshit. I don't owe the game a damn thing, and the game doesn't owe me anything. I've gotten out of the game just what I've put into it, no more, no less. I owe something to my friends and to my family, but not to any game.

About ten o'clock, Suzie and I and another couple went to Trader Vic's in the Plaza Hotel for dinner. It's a good place to go when you don't want to be bothered. It's not too crowded at that hour, and it's kind of dark and quiet, and people leave you alone. Of course, I wasn't left completely alone. A man sitting at a table across from ours brought me a couple of dollar bills to autograph; I thought I might keep one just in case I couldn't find a new job. When we finished dinner and got up to leave, two couples came in, saw me and did a double-take. "We just came over here," one of the men said, "because we couldn't get into Bachelors III. The line was too long. We just wanted to get a look at you. Good luck."

Well, hell, if business was that good at Bachelors III, at least I wasn't going to starve. As we came out of the Plaza a big black guy walked up to me and grabbed my hand. "Man," he said, "you got a lot of balls."

From Trader Vic's, we went to Bachelors III, and the

**27**

place was packed. Several of my teammates were there—Johnny Sample, the defensive captain, had come up from his home in Philadelphia—and several reporters, and several photographers, and I told the photographers to get the hell out. I didn't want them taking pictures inside the club. I didn't want to scare any customers away. You know, some of them may have been there with someone other than their own wife or their own husband—discussing business, probably—and I didn't want their pictures ending up in the *Daily News* just because I wasn't going to play football any more.

The next day, I took it kind of easy, and then on Sunday I flew out to Los Angeles to make one of the Emmy presentations. I gave the award to ABC for its coverage of the 1968 Olympic Games in Mexico; I really wanted to give it to NBC for *Heidi*, the show that cut off the end of the New York-Oakland regular-season game and prevented a national television audience from watching us collapse.

Then I flew up to Lake Tahoe on the California-Nevada border. I knew I wouldn't run into any undesirables up there. I was playing in a golf tournament sponsored by Harrah's Club, the gambling establishment, and among the other competitors were three of my fellow professional quarterbacks, Daryl Lamonica from Oakland and Don Meredith and Craig Morton from Dallas. It was perfectly all right for us to play golf on a course owned by professional gamblers, but I wasn't allowed to own a restaurant if professional gamblers happened to come in. It was logical.

Neither I nor my lawyers had any contact with Rozelle's

office while I was in Tahoe. I was getting resigned to the fact that I wasn't going to be able to play football.

At the blackjack table one night, I won a few pretty good hands, and when a young lady brought me a complimentary drink, I gave her a nice little tip, $15 or $20, something like that, I forget which.

"Gee, Joe," the girl said. "You shouldn't throw money away like that."

"Hell, that's nothing," I said. "You should have seen how much I threw away last week."

All across the country, newspapers kept running big headlines about me and Bachelors III. You'd think they could have found more important news that that. People began getting in touch with me and my lawyers about opening other Bachelors III establishments, maybe a chain of them from coast to coast. John Mackey, the great tight end of the Balitmore Colts, was interested in opening one in Baltimore; Jim Colclough, who was once with the Jets briefly, was interested in opening one in Boston; other people talked about Miami and about Los Angeles or San Diego. Bachelors III began to look like a helluva good investment. I've got to say one thing for Rozelle; he sure stirred up a lot of business for us.

We were getting a different kind of business in the New York club. The place hadn't been raided—no matter what Rozelle's sources told him—but the so-called undesirables had stopped coming in. Rozelle felt it was my influence that had gotten them to stop coming. Hell, I wish I were that strong. They're not stupid, those people. They weren't about to come into any place that was being watched day

**29**

and night by the D.A., the C.I.A., CBS and, I guess, the *Christian Science Monitor*.

We had a brand new set coming to Bachelors III—reporters and undercover cops. I've got nothing against undercover cops—well, hardly anything—but, damn, they're not good for business. For one thing, you can read them a mile away. For another, they ought to get better expense accounts. They sit and nurse a beer or two all night. They spend about as freely as sportswriters.

Then the stories began coming out in the magazines. *Life* was first. They called Bachelors III a "hoodlum-haunted" place. Well, they ought to know, because that week there were more *Life* reporters in the place than any other kind of people. Right at the beginning of their story, they talked about "tears welling from his big blue eyes," and *Life* could be in a little trouble if the rest of the story was just as accurate. My eyes are green, and they're damn nice eyes, and I'm hurt when people can't tell what color they are. I've heard that some of the undesirables were hurt, too; *Life* called them by the wrong nicknames. That's what I've heard; of course, I wouldn't know myself.

After *Newsweek* came out with a story that kind of reinforced the hints that had been in *Life*, *Sports Illustrated* took its shot. The first few paragraphs were all about some crap games that *Sports Illustrated* said took place in my Manhattan apartment. The magazine said the crap games were held in January and February of 1969. In January and February of 1969, after I got through with the Super Bowl, I was in Japan, Okinawa and Hawaii, visiting army hospitals; in San Diego, playing in a golf tournament; and in Miami, my winter home. I wasn't in New York for more than a couple of days during that whole period. *Sports Illustrated* never mentioned that fact; it might have made their story a little weaker.

Besides, there weren't any crap games in my apartment. My roommates don't know how to shoot craps, and we don't go lending out the apartment just to anybody who wants to use it. We may lend it out if a guy has a good reason—like if the girl has a roommate and the guy doesn't have a hotel room—but we don't lend it out for crap games. The story was just plain ridiculous, just an out-and-out smear job. And now the people from *Sports Illustrated* can't understand why I don't want to talk to their reporters and why I don't want to pose for their pictures. They think I'm being too touchy. Well, shit, if I did my job as sloppily as they did theirs in that crap-game story, I wouldn't be playing pro football, and they wouldn't want my picture.

The rumors that started floating around were as absurd as the magazine stories. The funniest rumor, I guess, was that the whole thing was a publicity stunt for Bachelors III or for my book or for my ego. Well, hell, if there's anything I don't have to look for, it's publicity. Everybody in the country, it seemed, was trying to get me to sit still for an interview before the Bachelors III thing broke, and I didn't need any stunt. If I'd been doing it for the book, I wouldn't have done it four or five months before publication; anybody who's ever seen me play knows I've got a better sense of timing than that. If I'd been doing it for Bachelors III, I'd have stayed in Bachelors III and out of football. Besides, the place was doing good business on its own; it didn't need all those cops and reporters in there. And if I was just doing it for personal publicity, do you think I would have returned to the Jets the same day the astronauts walked on the moon?

Another story going around was that I didn't want to play football, that my legs were shot and I couldn't move and I was just ducking out this way. That was plain stupid, too. If my legs were the real reason, I would have said so and collected on my Jet contract for the next two years. Sure, my legs were hurting, but they were hurting in 1968, too, and the year before, and I kept playing. I'm used to my legs hurting. I better be, because they're probably going to be hurting me the rest of my life, and I still intend to enjoy myself.

The wildest rumor of all was that the whole Bachelors III thing was just a cover-up to get me out of football gracefully, that I was really being kicked out because I had fixed the Buffalo and Denver games in 1968, the games in which I threw five interceptions each time. That's an insult. I'm too damn good a passer to throw five interceptions in a game I want to fix. Hell, you'd have to be an idiot to make it that obvious. If you want to throw a game, you don't have to allow a single pass to be intercepted. You just screw up one or two handoffs, and the running back can't handle them, and he fumbles the ball, and he takes the blame. Then maybe you throw a critical third-down pass a little low, and you let your punter come in and give the ball to the other team. You don't give it away yourself. That'd be stupid. The truth is that I was trying

32

to win those Buffalo and Denver games, but I was really trying to throw the game against Baltimore in the Super Bowl. I kept handing off high, but that damn Matt Snell wouldn't drop the ball, and I kept throwing low, but that silly Sauer kept making impossible catches. I bet you don't believe me. Well, then, how the hell can anyone believe all that bullshit the magazines wrote about me?

The week after I played golf at Harrah's Club. I went out to Seattle and played in a tournament sponsored by Pat Boone. Now, there's a real unsavory character. He's got the image of being an all-American boy, you know— white shoes, all that stuff—but actually he's a big *capo* in the Mafia. You ever heard of the Boone family? They're hard, man, real hard. When I finally settled with Rozelle, I promised I wouldn't associate any more with Pat Boone or Lawrence Welk or Bart Starr or any of those hoods.

For more than two weeks, I had no contact with Rozelle's office, and pressure kept building up, on him just as much as on me. I heard that the people at NBC, who had the rights to televise the American Football League games, weren't too happy about my retirement. I heard that the people who'd bought tickets to the New York Jets' season games and exhibition games, especially the exhibition against the Giants in New Haven, weren't too happy about my retirement. I heard that the owners of the Baltimore Colts and the Cleveland Browns and the Pittsburgh Steelers, who'd all transferred from the National Football League to the American, weren't too happy about my retirement. I can understand NBC and the fans getting upset, but I couldn't understand those owners being both-

**33**

ered. I mean, hell, now that I'm back playing, they're just going to have to get used to losing. They're not messing with those N.F.L. teams any more.

A lot of people wanted me to change my mind and come back and play, people I like, people I respect. My teammates respected my position completely—they had total faith in my honesty—but I knew they wanted me to play. We'd all put in too much hard work building a championship team to want to give it up so quickly.

I kept hoping we'd find some way I'd be able to play, but, damn, it just didn't look possible. Then, the last week in June, before I went out to Hollywood to appear in *Norwood*, my first movie, my lawyers heard from Rozelle. He wanted to sit down and talk with me. I was willing to talk. I wanted to hear what he had to say.

The day before my meeting with Rozelle, I went out to Shea Stadium to pick up some equipment I wanted to bring to the West Coast. Just in case I wanted a football and my shoes so that I could start getting in shape. I took a sauna out at Shea, and a few of my teammates were there, and we sat around and talked, and I could really feel how much I was going to miss them and miss the game if I didn't play. For several hours afterward, I could actually feel the sauna, the heat and the spirit of it, the laughs we'd all had in there, cutting up each other and cutting up Weeb after practice sessions.

The meeting with Rozelle was set for Thursday, June 26, and I didn't know in advance where it was going to be held. All I knew was that somebody was going to pick me up around one thirty outside my apartment. I got out

34

there at the right time, and there was Weeb, sitting in a station wagon driven by Bill Hampton, the equipment manager of the Jets. "Gee, Weeb," I wanted to say, "I'm sorry you got to put up with this." I didn't say it, but I thought it.

The fact that there was going to be a meeting had leaked out somehow—things kept leaking out all during the situation, and most of them were inaccurate—and there was a pack of reporters and cameramen waiting outside my building. Naturally, they wanted to know where the meeting was being held. Naturally, I told the reporters and the cameramen I didn't know, and, naturally, they didn't believe me. They decided to tail us, a car and a motorcycle, and we had a good chase, right out of a Steve McQueen movie. Bill Hampton lost the car that was trailing us pretty fast, but he couldn't shake the guy on the motorcycle. I told Bill, finally, just to pull over to the side and let the guy go past. The guy didn't go by. Instead, he stopped right behind us. When we didn't move, the guy parked his motorcycle in front of us, climbed off and walked back to me. "Look, Joe," he said, "I'm supposed to follow you wherever you go, but I don't enjoy it. It's not the sort of thing I like to do. I'm going to tell my office that you jumped out of the car and jumped into a cab, and I got mixed up and followed the car and lost you. Back me up on that, okay, if anybody asks you?"

He was a good guy—if his office is upset because he didn't track me to the meeting, I'll hire him to chase people for me—but, as it turned out, it wouldn't have made any difference if he had stuck with us. We pulled up on 57th

**35**

Street in front of the building where the New York Jets have their offices. We went in the entrance, and from the lobby Frank Ramos, the publicity director of the Jets, guided us out through a different door, onto Madison Avenue, where a different station wagon was waiting for us. Rozelle didn't want to take any chances on anybody finding out where the meeting was. The station wagon on Madison Avenue drove us to Rozelle's apartment house.

Jimmy Walsh met me and Weeb outside Rozelle's building, and then the three of us went up to see the commissioner. He hadn't arrived yet, and we waited in his study. When he showed up, with Jim Kensil, his assistant, Rozelle immediately opened up a large manila envelope and pulled out two photographs. They weren't mug shots of some new criminals I was supposed to know. They were photos of me in my Jets uniform.

"Could you sign these, Joe?" Rozelle said. "One's for my daughter, Ann. She's a real fan of yours. The other's for a friend of hers. Ann saw you playing softball the other day on the field near the 59th Street bridge and she almost went up to you and asked for your autograph then. She figured you'd ask her what her name was, and she was going to tell you—to prove that at least there's one Rozelle who doesn't hate you." I signed the pictures, and that was about the most constructive thing that came out of the whole meeting. Rozelle started off by telling me that the information in the magazine articles hadn't come from his office, but had been leaked by law enforcement agencies. I don't know which law enforcement agency was the main source, but whoever it was must have been giving

36

information to anybody who wanted it, whether the information was true or not.

Then Rozelle said that he had first heard stories in the fall of 1968 that I was under surveillance by law enforcement agencies, and that the investigation had something to do with some people I'd met in a bar on Mulberry Street.

I had just one question. "Where's Mulberry Street?" I said.

I was told that Mulberry Street is downtown in Manhattan, below Greenwich Village, around Chinatown. I'd never been on Mulberry Street in my life as far as I could remember. Hell, I never go below 57th Street—except when I want to visit the commissioner's office.

The meeting wasn't productive, mostly because I couldn't buy Rozelle's point of view and he couldn't buy mine. "I've done nothing wrong," I said.

"You say you've done nothing wrong," Rozelle said, "and we say you've done nothing illegal."

Rozelle pointed out to me other instances of what he called necessary double standards—for instance, the Supreme Court's rigid standards for its justices. (Somehow, it struck me kind of funny that Rozelle could, with a straight face, in all seriousness, compare professional football and the Supreme Court of the United States; I'm a football player, not a lawyer, but I don't think pro football is really quite on the same level as the Supreme Court.) "Just because other people have double standards," I said, "doesn't mean we have to."

Rozelle kept insisting that it was important for pro football to have special standards for its players because public faith in the game was essential. I could see his point, but I could also see my own. Personally, I hadn't done anything to violate the public faith.

"I've met some of those people," I said, when Rozelle read me the list of known gamblers who'd been seen in Bachelor III, "but I didn't know their backgrounds. Now that I know, I'm not going to talk to them. I'm going to stay away from them. And we're taking steps to keep Bachelors III clean. We've hired an investigator to provide us with security, to spot the sort of people who shouldn't be in there. The place is clean now, you admit that. Why should I have to sell out?"

Rozelle didn't seem to have any fresh facts that would change my opinion. Most of what he said actually seemed to be straight from the *Life* and *Newsweek* and *Sports Illustrated* stories. I don't know whether his office was feeding any information to the magazines—without his knowledge—but if they weren't, then they were getting their information from the magazines or from the same sources. And I knew those weren't good sources.

At one point during the meeting, which lasted about two hours, the phone next to Rozelle's chair rang. The commissioner picked it up. "Hello," he said. "Hello? Hello?"

He hung up the phone. "That was pretty damn stupid of me," he said. Obviously, some newspaper or television station had called, and once Rozelle answered the phone they didn't have to ask any questions. They knew where we were meeting.

At another point, when the conversation was pretty serious, when both Rozelle and I were really trying to find some common ground for discussion, Weeb pulled a little card out of his pocket and held it up. It said: Damned if I know.

"I show that to anybody who asks me any questions about what's going on," said Weeb, with a big grin. I knew I could count on him to be helpful.

The meeting broke up without anything being resolved and without any plans for a specific future meeting. Rozelle said he might come out to California to talk to me while I was filming, but that he wasn't certain.

The next day, I flew to Boston to attend a football clinic and to talk about a Boston Bachelors III with Jim Colclough, and right after that, I left for California for the movie role. While I was in California, I had time to just sit and think about the whole situation, and the more I thought about it, the more upset I became. It was so senseless, so hypocritical. All I'd done was say hello to some people who like to back their opinions with cash. I hadn't talked football with them; I hadn't told them how to bet; I'd just treated them decently and politely, the way I'd treat any customer, the way I'd want anyone to treat me. I was in the restaurant business, and I was enjoying it, and there was no way in the whole world I could control who came in and out of that restaurant. There are laws against kicking people out of public establishments. Maybe some guys had placed bets over the phones in Bachelors III, but, hell, bets have been placed over half the pay phones in New York, and neither I nor the commissioner can do anything about that. Goldang, why did the commissioner have to act so holy? He knows just as well as I do that millions of dollars are bet every week on professional football games. That's one of the reasons the game's so popular. If he ever succeeded in eliminating all betting on pro football, he'd also eliminate a good share of the interest in the game. He'd be killing his own box office. I could understand him not wanting me to bet—that's obvious grounds for suspension—but I hadn't bet, on my team or against my team. Rozelle knew that, and I knew that.

While I was in California, Jimmy Walsh had a few discussions with Rozelle's office. Nothing much was accomplished in those talks, but the groundwork was laid for me to meet again with Rozelle when I returned. I thought he sincerely wanted to find a solution. "I'd be a damn fool if I didn't want to see you in football," Rozelle had said during our previous meeting. "You're the biggest name we've got." I felt he meant it.

Just before I left California to return to New York, a story broke that I was going to report to the Jets' training camp on Sunday, July 13, the day all veterans had to report. The story suggested that I was going to show up without selling Bachelors III and that I was just going in order to be suspended so that I could then start court action against professional football. Well, hell, that was considered. So was playing football in Canada considered. So was barnstorming with my own team, playing exhibitions. A lot of things have to be considered in a situation like this, but the main thing was that I wanted to play football and I wanted to play in the American Football League, against the best competition.

The newspaper stories were wrong, as usual. The *Daily News* was positive I'd be in training camp Sunday morning. So were a lot of writers and television people. Damn, I really felt badly about making all those guys get up so early on a Sunday morning and go out to the Jets camp in Hempstead, Long Island, and wait for me to show up. They'd all been so nice and friendly to me.

On Sunday night, after I hadn't reported, I was in Bachelors III, and several of my teammates came in to see me. Curley Johnson and Johnny Sample and Pete Lammons and a bunch of others came in, and it was good to see them. Curley always makes me laugh. When I was a rookie, at training camp in Peekskill, New York, I got a phone call one day, and this girl said to me, "Hi, dahlin'. Ah'd love to get together with you." She talked a pretty good game, and I agreed to meet her downtown in Peekskill. When I showed up at the meeting place, there was no girl around. There were just a few of the guys—and Curley Johnson. "Hi, dahlin'," he said.

Damn Texans.

I could tell the guys really wanted me to play, and I told them I wanted to play, I wanted to find a solution. If it had been only me, if the situation hadn't affected anyone else, I'm pretty sure I would've stayed out of football. I would've maintained my ownership of Bachelors III. But my friends and my family and my teammates were all being affected; people who'd invested in my businesses were being hurt; people who'd been damn good to me

**41**

were being hurt. I didn't owe football anything, but I owed all these people something. I wanted to get back in football.

The next day, Monday, I met with Rozelle for four hours, just the two of us, head-to-head. If nothing else, I came away feeling that he knew I'd done nothing wrong and that he had nothing against me personally. He told me all the magazine articles had put him—and me—in a bind. He explained there was no way he could back down; I had to sell my interest in Bachelors III if I wanted to play football.

One of the points of disagreement between Rozelle and me had been over Bobby Van and Ray Abruzzese. Rozelle had gotten what he called bad reports on both of them. The reports were wrong, dead wrong. Sure, Bobby knew a lot of people whose last names ended with vowels, but, hell, his name ended with a vowel, too, till he shortened it from Vannuchi to Van. He knew the kind of people who frequented East Side bars because he'd been working for about ten years in East Side bars. And Ray, shoot, Ray is so damned friendly, he talks with everybody and smiles with everybody and just enjoys himself. I knew—I was absolutely positive—that Bobby and Ray hadn't done anything wrong and that Rozelle's information—he called it information, not fact—was wrong. Monday night, I brought Ray and Bobby back with me to see the commissioner.

Ray, of course, got the commissioner laughing. At one point, the question came up of me giving away my share of Bachelors III. "Yeah, Pete," Ray said to Rozelle, "make him just give it away. I'll take it off his hands." We all laughed.

Ray and Bobby explained their positions well enough to the commissioner to convince him, I think, that they'd done nothing wrong, either. They must have because, after I talked with Rozelle over the telephone on Tuesday and Wednesday and Jimmy Walsh went to see him a few times, the commissioner dropped any objection to my friendship with Ray and Bobby. That was a major point; I wasn't going to break off my friendship with Ray and Bobby under any circumstances, no matter how much I wanted to play football.

On Wednesday night, I went out to see my teammates and explain my position to them. I made a brief statement, giving them all the background, and they asked me a few questions. One of the guys wanted to know if Bobby Van had any convictions, and I told them he hadn't. Most of the guys were glad to see me and just kidded me and wanted to know if I could get them good jobs, after football, with the mob. I promised them each a territory for themselves.

I picked up my world championship ring, and, damn, it's a beautiful thing. It's got a cluster of diamonds in the middle, and it's really tasteful. I'd seen the world championship rings the Green Bay Packers had won, and you had to be at least the size of a defensive tackle to wear them. I bet Vince Lombardi picked them out because he knew anybody who could carry one of those rings would have to be in shape. I was really happy with ours. I'd been insisting, from the day we won the Super Bowl, that we

**43**

should have the best championship rings ever made, and I think we got them.

On Thursday, Mike Bite, my lawyer—of all people—came up with a compromise solution to the situation. I hate to admit it was Mike's idea, because there won't be any living with him from now on. He'll probably want a bonus contract. His solution was that I sell out my share in Bachelors III in New York, but that I retain the right to invest in other Bachelors III restaurants in other parts of the country. Our argument certainly seemed legitimate. There was nothing even slightly wrong with those other Bachelors III; nobody undesirable had gone into places that didn't even exist yet. I didn't see how Rozelle could object to that. I also wanted the right to sell my share of the New York Bachelors III to Ray Abruzzese or Bobby Van or anyone outside my family and my lawyers who could be approved by the State Liquor Authority.

Friday morning, July 18, Jimmy Walsh met with Rozelle again and presented our compromise proposal. The commissioner accepted it. Then Jimmy and Mike and I met for lunch. I still wasn't convinced I was doing the right thing. I still felt bad about getting out of Bachelors III; the place never had been raided, nobody had been arrested in there and no one had come up with any proof of wrongdoing on the part of my friends or me. Mike and Jimmy kept assuring me that I was doing the right thing, that I wasn't surrendering my principle, that I was just losing a battle to win the war. They had a helluva time convincing me. It was against all my instincts. But, finally, they won. They persuaded me to sell.

**44**

Jimmy arranged for us to meet with Rozelle in the afternoon, and as we came out of the little luncheonette where we'd been eating, we jumped into a taxi. The driver was a man named Marty Liptone. As we got in, the driver glanced around. "Football player," he said. "Joe Namath. Screw Pete Rozelle. Don't give in."

Mike and Jimmy almost died. They thought all their arguments had gone to waste. They thought I was going to change my mind again. "How many cabs are there in New York?" Mike asked the driver.

"About twelve thousand."

"And we have to get you."

We all went to Rozelle's office, and the commissioner reviewed the situation, and I stuck out my hand and shook his. We were agreed. I was coming back to football, and I was selling my share of Bachelors III in New York, and I was free to invest in other Bachelors III in other parts of the country.

At least for a while, I wasn't going to be going into Bachelors III in Manhattan; we didn't make any permanent agreement on that, but it didn't make too much difference right then, anyway. I was going to report to training camp on Sunday, and once I got to training camp I'd be keeping an eleven o'clock curfew, and, hell, I never used to go into Bachelors III before eleven, anyway.

Right after the meeting and after a brief press conference to announce the settlement, I flew off to California to film a final scene for my movie. The next morning, while I was sweating in the desert, playing an ex-marine hitchhiking home, the newspapers were all saying that I had

**45**

capitulated to Rozelle. That was bullshit. I'd given in more than I'd wanted to, but I hadn't sold out my principle. I had a pretty good feeling that Bobby and Ray and I were all going to be in business together somewhere. And I felt that I'd been vindicated, that all those dumb rumors about me had been proven false.

When I phoned Weeb to tell him that I was coming out to camp on Sunday, he asked me if there was anything he could do for me. I guess he was willing to put up with me for another year.

"Yeah, there is, Weeb," I said. "Could you put an air conditioner, a color television and an ice box in my room in the dorm?"

"Well, Joe," he said, very seriously, "we've got air conditioning in there already, but I don't know what I can do about those other things."

Hey, Weeb, I was only kidding.

On Sunday, I flew back in from California. Mike and Jimmy and Jim Hudson—coming out of *his* retirement to join me—picked me up at the airport and rode with me to the training camp. I arrived around dinner time, when most of the players were gone—there was just a group of reporters around; I didn't have too much to say to them— and Hudson and I went up to our room on the tenth floor of the Hofstra College dormitory.

The first guy to come into our room was Curley Johnson.

"Hi, dahlin'," he said.

I was home.

I was back with the champions of the whole world.

**46**

# 2

Who'd They Think
They Were Messing
With — the Rams?

■▬▬▬▬▬▬▬■

The day after we beat the Oakland Raiders for the 1968
American Football League championship, one of my
friends came running up to me. "Hey, Joe," he said. "You
hear the spread for the Super Bowl game?"

"No," I said. "What's the spread?"

"Seventeen points," he said. "Seventeen mother points."

"Hell," I said. "That's crazy. We should only be favored
by nine or ten."

I wasn't serious, of course. I knew that Baltimore was
going to be favored over us. But when I heard that they
were favored by seventeen points, I couldn't believe it.
I couldn't believe anybody would be dumb enough to give
us seventeen points.

Sure, I knew the Baltimore Colts had a great team. I knew some people were saying they had the greatest team in the history of professional football. They'd only lost two games in two years, so they had to be pretty damn good. But I knew we had a great team, too. We were the New York Jets, man, and you just couldn't give the New York Jets seventeen points. Who'd they think the Colts were going to be playing—the Los Angeles Rams or the Cleveland Browns or one of those teams?

Back in the middle of the season, when it began to look as though we had a good shot at the American Football League title, I started thinking a little about playing against Baltimore. I was really looking forward to it; it was like a dream game to me. The Colts had always been my favorite team before I began playing pro ball myself, and Johnny Unitas had been my favorite player. I used to think Johnny was the best quarterback of all time. I still rate him one of the top two.

I didn't get much time to think about the Colts during the year because I had to be thinking more about the Oakland Raiders and the Kansas City Chiefs. We were pretty sure we'd end up playing either the Raiders or the Chiefs in the American Football League championship game, and I wasn't looking beyond that game. I didn't have any strong opinion about exactly how good the Colts were. I don't judge a team until I've watched their game movies, until I've studied what they can do and what they can't do. I don't just believe what somebody writes in the newspapers. I've met a few sportwriters who can't read without moving their lips.

**50**

For a few days after the Oakland game, while sports-writers all over the country were telling everybody how bad Baltimore was going to beat us, I just relaxed and enjoyed the feeling of being a part of the champions of the American Football League. The day after New Year's, we flew to Fort Lauderdale to start getting ready for the Super Bowl. When I was a teenager, I thought about joining the Air Force—it looked like one good way for me to stay out of the Pennsylvania steel mills—and becoming a pilot. I still think I'd like to learn how to fly, but I don't enjoy commercial planes. I don't enjoy them at all. On the way down to Florida, I managed to calm my nerves with a few Johnnie Walker tranquilizers.

From the airport, we drove over to the Galt Ocean Mile, the same hotel the Green Bay Packers had stayed in the year before, and Jim Hudson and I checked into our room, the Governor's Suite, the same room Vince Lombardi, the Green Bay coach, had lived in the year before. I think Lombardi's a helluva coach, and he's always said nice things about me, but I'm not sure he would have approved of everything I did in his old room the week before the Super Bowl.

All year, wherever the Jets went, Hudson and I took a suite. Just so the club wouldn't go broke, we shared the difference in price between a regular double room and a suite. I actually need a suite, because I get a lot of visitors, people who want to come up and talk about football and things like that—you'd be surprised how many girls there are who like to talk football in my hotel room—and I don't like to disturb Hudson. It's good having Jim around,

**51**

though, because he's a married man, and a lot of girls wouldn't feel safe in a hotel room with just a bachelor. As long as I've got Jim around as a chaperone, all the girls feel safe.

The very first morning in Fort Lauderdale, I had a couple of visitors, but they didn't want to come up to my room, and they didn't want to talk football. They said they were law enforcement officials. On our last trip to Miami, to play the Dolphins, some distinguished citizen had threatened to kill me. (Later, when all those stories were going around that I was the new headman of the Cosa Nostra—hell, I'm not even eligible; I just *look* Italian—this gentleman was rumored to be one of my closest friends. I don't think that's a very nice way to show friendship.) I lived through that previous trip, and the two visitors said they hoped I'd do just as well on this one. "A routine checkup," one of the guys told me. He was very happy about the particular room I'd picked. He said that, because of the position of my balcony, anybody who wanted to shoot me would have to fire from a wide-open spot on the beach behind the hotel. "There's nothing to worry about," said the investigator. "If he shoots you, he can't possibly get away." That really made me feel a lot better.

I've got to admit that I'm not one of the biggest fans of the law enforcement agencies these days. I mean, I don't mind them tapping my phones. I don't even mind them playing the tapes for every tourist who walks into their offices. I just wish to hell that they'd pay their share of the phone bill. That's only fair.

**52**

It wasn't nice of the law enforcement people to send complete strangers to talk to me in Fort Lauderdale. The least they could've done was send the guys who'd been tailing me during the season. I'm pretty sure they started keeping me company right after we lost a couple of games to Buffalo and Denver. It was nothing personal, but, as I mentioned earlier, I had five passes intercepted in each of those games, and the D.A. or the C.I.A. or somebody like that got a little curious. Nothing serious. They just checked all my bank deposits. I don't blame them, I guess. I know that some people actually do bet on professional football games. Guys kid me now and then: "C'mon, Joe, you want to make fifty thousand dollars this weekend?" and I kid them right back, "Who do I have to kill?" and they just laugh. They're only fooling around, but some people just don't have any sense of humor.

Not too long after the Denver game, Ray Abruzzese, my roommate, and I began to get the feeling that we were being trailed and that our phone in our apartment was being tapped. Ray, who used to play for the Jets, thought maybe the phone was being tapped by an irate husband, but I told him it probably wasn't that serious, probably just the C.I.A. We were both pretty amused, but we stopped cracking funny jokes on the phone about point spreads.

Then I had to go out of town for a road game. We were taking a ridiculously early chartered flight, about ten o'clock in the morning, and Ray and I slept through the alarm. We didn't wake up till about nine thirty. We got dressed quick and I just grabbed a toothbrush, figuring I'd pick up some clothes out of town, and Ray started

**53**

driving me to the airport. I kept hoping that the plane had taken off. I knew I'd get fined for missing the flight, but I was more worried about keeping everybody waiting. I knew I could catch a later plane.

We were about twenty minutes from the airport when, suddenly, Ray started cursing like crazy. "Why didn't that mother wake us up?" Ray said.

"Who you talking about?" I said.

"That mother that's following us," Ray said, nodding at the rear-view mirror. "Shit, he knew what time we had to be at the airport, the bastard. Why didn't he call us up? Why didn't he wake us?" Ray was really mad at the guy. He went down at least a notch or two in Ray's estimation that day.

When I wasn't busy talking to the law that first morning in Fort Lauderdale, I was down in the Imperial Room of the Galt Ocean Mile attending a team meeting and getting my first look at the Baltimore movies. Like always, I only watched their defensive team, the guys I'd be facing, and, I'll tell you, I enjoyed that show as much as a good Lee Marvin movie. I saw what the Colts could do and what they couldn't do, and I liked what I saw. Some people were saying that the Jets'd be scared of the Colt defense. Scared, hell—the only thing that scared me was that they might change their defense.

What I liked best was the Baltimore safety blitz. Lots of times, just before the snap or on the snap, they moved their two safeties, Rick Volk and Jerry Logan, up to fill in the gaps between the linebackers. Sometimes, one safety would blitz—shoot through and try to get the quarterback

—and, sometimes, the other one would blitz. No matter who blitzed, they had to leave part of the middle open. I knew I could hit my wide receivers slanting in. (Of course, I knew I was going to get hit, too. You get hit almost every time on those blitzes—and I don't enjoy getting hit—but it's worth it to have those receivers open.)

The more I saw of the Baltimore movies, the better I felt. Cleveland and Minnesota and Los Angeles were just plain dumb against the blitz. The Browns kept trying to run through the packed Baltimore line. The Rams used some quick sideline patterns that didn't disrupt the blitz at all. The Vikings didn't do a damn thing to throw the Baltimore defense off balance; as far as I could tell, they never varied their count, never took a real long count or a real quick count to break the rhythm of the Colts. I'd been telling people all year that the American Football League had caught up to the National Football League and people kept telling me I was wrong. Well, I was wrong. We'd already passed them in a lot of things.

I just prayed that the Colts would blitz us. If they did, I figured, they were dead. Our backs are just the best there are at picking up a blitz. Matt Snell and Bill Mathis are fantastic, and Emerson Boozer keeps getting better and better, both blocking and reading defenses. And our ends, Don Maynard and George Sauer and Pete Lammons, can smell a blitz a mile away. They've got a whole bunch of little signals to change their patterns; like, if Maynard winks at me, he means he's going to run an I pattern. In the 1968 season, we handled the blitz like crazy. Against Miami, we completed five touchdown passes, and all five

**55**

came against the blitz. Anybody that's ever played in the American Football League will tell you not to blitz against New York. Of course, the Colts didn't know that; they didn't have any regulars—just one substitute—who'd played in the American Football League. We had three or four guys on our club who'd spent some time with the Colts before they moved up in class.

After our first look at the movies, we went to the practice field for a light workout. Somebody told me that I'd been assigned the same locker Mickey Mantle used in spring training with the Yankees. Mickey and I are pretty good friends; between us, we've got almost one good pair of legs.

Our uniforms were hanging in the locker room. Because we'd been designated the visiting team in the Super Bowl, we had our white uniforms. It was only right that the good guys should be wearing white; besides, I always wear white football shoes, and I like my outfits to be co-ordinated. All the omens looked good—white uniforms plus we were playing the Super Bowl game on the twelfth, my uniform number.

The day after the F.B.I. came to see me, I had another fun visitor. Dr. James Nicholas paid a house call to my suite. Nick the Knife is a specialist. He specializes in cutting up my knees and sticking needles into me. He's really painless. I mean, he doesn't feel any pain at all. I had him look me over pretty good. My right thumb was aching; it started hurting in the second game of the season, and I'd been having trouble with it, on and off, ever since. Normally, when you hold your hand straight in front of you, palm out, you can bring the thumb down horizontal to the ground. I could just bring it down to a forty-five-degree angle. Dr. Nicholas told me to keep a heat pack around it whenever I could. There had been some talk about shooting the thumb with a painkiller, but I'm funny about my whole right arm. I don't want anybody to do anything to it. I want it to stay just natural. It takes good care of me, and I take good care of it, no arm wrestling or weight lifting or anything like that. The tricep muscle, the muscle leading from the back of the shoulder to the back of the elbow, had acted up on me a few days before the Oakland game; I'd felt a sharp, sudden pain. The pain went away and didn't bother me again, but just to be safe, I told Dr. Nicholas to look at the arm. It looked fine to him.

Then Dr. Nicholas got to his fun. He took a needle three inches long, and after rubbing some antiseptic and some Novocaine on my right knee, jabbed the needle in about two inches deep. For thirty seconds, he drained fluid off my knee. He took about two ounces of yellowish fluid. The color was a good sign; if the fluid comes out red, it means something's torn inside.

Dr. Nicholas tried hard not to hurt me with the needle, but I guess I must've looked like I was in agony. "Hey, Doc," Hudson called, from across the room, "you know something? You're a sadist. You really enjoy this work, don't you?"

Nick got very offended. "You have absolutely no respect for the medical profession," he told Hudson. "You have no respect at all." It struck me so funny: Hudson was putting the needle to Nick, for a change, and Nick was hurt. I almost fell off the couch laughing.

"Damn, Doc," Hudson said, "I'm sorry. I was only kidding."

Dr. Nicholas accepted Hudson's apology. Then he told me to take it easy, and I promised him I wouldn't get into any sprint races against anybody.

The days leading up to the Super Bowl game passed quickly. I was busy, debating Lou Michaels, sleeping through our picture session, keeping Jimmy Fazio out of bankruptcy. I practiced, too. I practiced damn hard, and I watched Baltimore movies in my room, as well as at our team meetings. I loved what the projector showed me; the one-eyed monster tells no lies. I guess my teammates felt the same way. "Damn, Joe, we better stop watching those movies," Pete Lammons said to me, after one meeting, "or we're gonna get overconfident." I cracked up laughing. Then I realized Pete was right; I wondered which one of us was going to call up the Colts and tell them they didn't have a chance.

Three days before the game, after I got my right knee drained again and had some pain reliever shot into my left knee for the tendon there that's always inflamed, I went down to the Miami Springs Villas to receive an award from the Touchdown Club as the outstanding player in pro football. I knew the place pretty well. Eastern Airlines stewardesses train there; I've done some training there myself during the off-season.

"We're going to win Sunday," I told the people at the Touchdown Club dinner. "I'll guarantee you."

I was just telling those people the truth. I know I'm not allowed to bet on football games, but, what the hell, all those people were nice enough to give me an award, I figured I'd be nice enough to give them a good tip. They should have mortgaged their houses and put everything on the Jets. Hell, they could have bought their own llama rugs and their own fur coats. Instead, some of them thought Namath's a real joker. I don't joke about football. I don't joke about the game.

I honestly felt that we had a better team. Judging from the movies, as I said before, I wasn't too impressed by the Baltimore defense. Come to think of it, judging from a couple of their games I saw on television, I wasn't too impressed by their offense, either. And I felt that we had a stronger team physically. Almost all of us were under thirty, and a lot of us were twenty-four and twenty-five and twenty-six. Yet, because we'd started with the Jets when the Jets were down, we had just as much playing experience as the older Colts. I bet I'd thrown almost as many passes in four seasons as Earl Morrall had thrown in thirteen. I felt Maynard, Sauer and Lammons, as a group, were better receivers than Baltimore's Jimmy Orr, Willie Richardson and John Mackey; I felt Snell and Boozer were better runners than Baltimore's Tom Matte and Jerry Hill. I didn't see any way they were better than us.

I study football, and I understand it—well, I understand some of it—and when I say we're a better football team, you can go to sleep on that. I know the better team doesn't always win, but when you've got the better team plus

**59**

eighteen points—the price had gone up a point by then; there must've been a lot of stupid people running to the bookmakers—it's like stealing.

Still, some people said I was just shooting my mouth off, I was just whistling in the dark, I was just trying to act confident so that my teammates wouldn't be afraid of the Colts. Now, that's absurd. I know my teammates, and they're not afraid of anything. What's going to frighten Gerry Philbin? He'd tackle a tank. And Winston Hill and Dave Herman and Johnny Sample and Verlon Biggs and Jim Hudson, shoot, those guys don't scare. I'm the only guy on the whole team who doesn't go around looking for physical contact. And, once in a while, Emerson Boozer'll stay back just to keep me company.

The Colts didn't act any smarter than the people who bet on them. "When he gets a little older," Baltimore's Billy Ray Smith said about me, "he'll get humility." He was just mouthing words. He never met me. He didn't know me. He didn't know what the hell he was talking about. Who says when I get older I'll get humility?

Two days before the game, my father and my brother Bob came down to Florida from Beaver Falls. My father took time off from his job in the steel mill; my brother took time off from his bar and grill in Monaca, just outside Beaver Falls. Neither of them took time off to watch me lose. My mother was supposed to make the trip, too, but she gets very nervous about flying and she wasn't feeling too well, so I told her to stay home and watch us win on television. I didn't want to take any chance on her getting hijacked to Havana and missing the game.

**60**

The night before the game, after our ten o'clock team buffet, a ritual before road games, I went up to my suite. I didn't go up alone. I took some Baltimore films with me. About eleven o'clock, Clive Rush, our offensive coach, stopped by my room, the regular pre-game bed-check. He saw I had the projector set up. "See anything new?" he asked me. "Same stuff," I said. Clive didn't have to worry about me missing curfew. Weeb Ewbank had put in a curfew starting Tuesday night, and just like everybody else on the team, I made curfew every night. It wasn't that I felt I had to get to bed so early—I can't fall asleep before two or three o'clock, no matter what—but I knew that if I were missing, Weeb wouldn't be able to sleep, and I wanted him fresh and rested for the game.

I had only one real problem the night before the game. Jim Hudson had deserted me. His wife had come down for the game, and he'd moved into another room with her, leaving me all alone. I hate to watch movies by myself. Maybe I'm afraid of the dark. I was just plain lucky. I found a friendly young lady who wasn't afraid of the dark to keep me company. She took notes and things like that. It was awfully nice of her to help me out, especially since, she told me later, her father had made a big bet on the Colts. But she said that she'd bet on the Jets and, damn, she was such a good girl that if she'd lost that bet I would have covered it for her. I knew she had a sure thing, anyway.

It was a nice peaceful way to spend the eve of a game. It really calmed me down. I'm supposed to be a big swinger, but I can enjoy a Saturday-night movie just as

**61**

much as anything else. I got plenty of sleep. I was wide awake for breakfast at eleven o'clock. I didn't feel like eating. I was looking forward to the game too much. I was looking forward to a lot of fun.

On the bus going to the Orange Bowl in Miami, I thought about the game, thought about specific situations. I didn't exactly daydream, but I could almost visualize certain things happening. I could see Maynard flying down the sidelines, for instance, sprinting beyond the man covering him, breaking into the clear, and I could see me lofting the ball, over the defender, into Maynard's arms, and I could see Maynard scoring. I could see the safety blitz, too. It looked beautiful to me.

In the dressing room, Jeff Snedeker, our trainer, wrapped tape all around my right knee. Then, just as he had for every game for four years, he taped a steel-and-rubber brace to the knee. Personally, I don't think the brace does anything except make it a little more difficult for me to move around, but Weeb thinks it does some good and Jeff goes along with him. I don't want to hurt their feelings.

After Jeff helped me off the table, I walked back into the locker room and listened to Weeb's pre-game speech. I don't need a speech to get me up for a big game. I just half-listened. Weeb reminded a few of the guys that the Colts had gotten rid of them and that they now had a chance to get even.

I went out on the field, loose and relaxed. I just had the normal butterflies, just enough inner tension to get the adrenaline flowing good. The way I figured, I didn't have anything to worry about. It was just going to be another triumph for clean living.

The Colts kicked off to us, and on our first play from scrimmage, I called our shift, our left guard moving over between our center and our right guard. I just wanted to let the Colts know right away that we had the shift, that they were going to have to adjust their defenses to us, that we were going to act and they'd have to react. I just wanted them to realize they weren't playing with children.

I wasn't too surprised by the way the game went. I was a little surprised how well the Colts moved the ball against our defense the first couple of times they got the ball. I watched from the sidelines and I thought, "Well, hell, maybe they're gonna score a touchdown or two." It didn't worry me. It just meant we'd have to score a few more.

I don't think we played a particularly great game, not by our standards. We played pretty much the way we'd played in our better games all year. Of course, any game's a great game when you win, but I know my own performance wasn't anything special. The second time we had the ball, I sent Don Maynard out on a fly pattern, and it worked almost the way I'd been seeing it in my head. Don streaked down the sidelines and he got past Jerry Logan and I lofted the ball downfield and Don stretched for it, and the goldang ball sailed about two inches beyond his reach. When the game ended, Don came up to me, shaking his head. "Durn, I'm sorry, Joe," he said.

"What for?" I said.

"Well, shucks," he said, "if my leg hadn't been hurt, I would have got to that."

"Your leg still bothering you?" I said. Maynard's leg had really been killing him the last four, five weeks of the season.

"Yeah," he said.

Hell, if I'd known that, I would have thrown the ball two inches shorter.

The next play right after that, George Sauer was wide open on the left, and I threw the ball five yards over his head. Just a miserable pass. I had trouble throwing to my left on and off all day; sometimes, I'd throw perfect to my left and, other times, I'd just get my thumb and my grip all messed up and throw terrible. In the third quarter, my thumb got hit, and it hurt like hell, but I came out of the game for just one series of downs.

Our plays against the Baltimore blitz worked beautifully. Every time I came up to the line of scrimmage, I thought to myself, Please let them blitz, please. And they did. I didn't complete every pass play against the blitz. I missed two or three times, but we hurt them a lot more than they hurt us. On one of those misses, George Sauer broke clean, and he was just wide open, but I couldn't find him. He was in a dead spot in my vision. We had a communication problem on the play. I thought George was going to go to the inside, and George thought I was expecting him to go to the outside. I had to run with the ball that time, and I got tackled, and we had to settle for a field goal. We should've had a touchdown; Sauer could've picked up thirty yards on that play if I'd spotted him.

I must have called more than a third of our plays—at least half of our running plays—at the line of scrimmage, looking over the Baltimore defense, anticipating their moves, deciding what to do. It got to the point where I was just telling the guys in the huddle, "Check with me," meaning I'd call the play at the line. There was no sense wasting time calling a play in the huddle, because I knew I'd change it to a better play with an automatic, an audible, at the line. During the weeks after the Super Bowl, I started learning how to play chess, with pawns and rooks and bishops, but I was really learning during the game. You don't have much time to stop and appreciate what you're doing while you're playing a football game, but it's the same sort of strategy as a chess match.

I can't say enough about how good our guys were in picking up the plays at the line of scrimmage. I mean, it's really a hard thing for them. When I change a play at the line, they've got to drive the play they've been thinking about from their minds and they've got to replace it with a new one and, in a few seconds, they've got to be ready for a different assignment, maybe on a different snap count, maybe in a whole different direction. Our guys didn't bust one play all day, didn't miss a single assignment as far as I could tell, never jumped offsides or anything. Two or three years earlier, if I'd tried calling all those audibles, before we really knew each other, our guys would have been flopping all over the field, getting in each other's way, missing blocks, fouling up everything.

**65**

But, against Baltimore, their coordination, their discipline, was just fantastic. It was a bitch of a test, and every guy on our club passed it.

I varied our snap count all through the game. Sometimes we went on the first sound; the ball was snapped to me the first sound I made. Sometimes we went on the color I called, sometimes on the first number and sometimes on the third and sometimes on the sixth. I had a rhythm of my own going, an erratic rhythm inside my head, and it was upsetting the Baltimore rhythm, just like I knew it would.

Take our first touchdown—hell, our *only* touchdown; it just seems like we had more. We were down near the Baltimore goal line, and when I saw Lou Michaels come on the field, I knew positively that the Colts were going into a tight five-one defense. From watching the movies, I knew that with Michaels in there on a short-yardage situation the Colts wouldn't use any other defense. Up until then, as far as I can remember, I hadn't called any plays on the first sound because, when the play's on the first sound—when I say, "Now!"—there's no way I can check off the play at the line of scrimmage. Against the Colts, obviously, I liked to be able to check off. But the first play with Michaels on the field, I said, "We'll go on the first sound." I called a 19-straight, a handoff to Snell, and Matt bounced around the left side and scored. We had the Colts off balance then, and they never really got their balance back.

Weeb and some other people said afterward that I called a perfect game, but that's not true. I made a couple

66

of mistakes. I threw one pass that I shouldn't have thrown. In the third quarter, on a third-down-and-long situation, I threw to Pete Lammons on a hook pattern, and Jerry Logan almost intercepted. I should never have released the ball. I was really forcing the pass. But even though I did a bad thing, I did one thing right on the play. I kept the ball outside Lammons. I saw Logan lying in the grass, wanting to go for the ball, so I threw on the far side of Lammons, away from Logan. Well, Logan lunged for the ball and touched it, but he couldn't hold it. If I'd thrown right at Lammons, Logan would have intercepted. He might even have run the ball back for a touchdown. I still don't know why I threw the ball; I should have eaten it.

I threw two other passes during the game that looked like they might've been intercepted, but I don't consider them mistakes. One Lenny Lyles reached for and missed and Sauer caught, and the other was a miserable end-over-end job that Don Shinnick of the Colts knocked down. I watched the films afterward, and they were good smart passes; they weren't going to be intercepted. If I'd thrown that damn pass right, the one Shinnick knocked down, we'd have gained twenty yards; Sauer and I had both read the Baltimore defense just right, and then I flopped the ball through the air like a girl.

My only other mistake came in the fourth quarter. When we were leading, 16-0, I ran a play on the first sound. At that stage, when we were trying to use up the clock, I shouldn't have done that. It was just plain stupid on my part. But, outside of that and the pass to Lammons, I guess I've got to admit that Weeb was right.

Hell, our whole club came pretty close to being perfect, which didn't surprise me at all. That's the way we play. We don't expect to make any mistakes. Jim Hudson was practically sick after the game because he'd missed a tackle on Tom Matte when Matte got off a long run right after our touchdown. "I had him, I had him at the line of scrimmage," Hudson said. "I was gonna kill him and I closed my eyes and I missed him. Damn." We'd just won the championship of the whole world, and Hudson was almost sick because he'd missed one tackle.

I dont want to take anything away from the Colts. Taking the world championship is enough. They're a helluva football team. Matte's a great runner, and they hit hard, and they play clean, tough football. But, just like I'd been saying all along and everybody'd been laughing, the Jets are a great football team, too. People say Sauer and Maynard and Lammons are good, and that's not half enough to describe them. And our defense was just beyond belief. The people who came to the Super Bowl saw a great defensive team, but it wasn't the Colts.

All of our guys really hit. On our first series of plays, Rick Volk tackled Matt Snell, and Matt hit him so hard Volk was shook up the rest of the game. He wound up in the hospital with a concussion. When I heard about that, I was really sorry he'd been hurt. I mean it. Sure, Volk was trying to get to me and kill me on the blitzes, but that's football, that's his job. The name of the game is kill the quarterback, and Volk was just playing the game. On the field and off the field are two different things. I hate to see anybody get hurt. Especially me, of course.

**68**

The only thing that really upset me all day was that, after the game was over and we'd won, 16-7, we didn't have any champagne in our locker room. That was just plain ridiculous. Weeb and Milt Woodard, the president of the American Football League, said that it wouldn't look right on television for us to be drinking, that it'd be bad for our image, bad for the sport, a bad influence on children. They were acting childish themselves. It was pure hypocrisy, and hypocrisy hurts our image a lot more than a couple of glasses of champagne. We were the champions, man, the best in the world, and we had Cokes and Gatorade to drink. The whole thing left a bad taste in my mouth. I washed it out later with Johnnie Walker.

I had some night. I stayed up till the sun rose the next day. Hell, I'd been getting too much sleep all week, anyway. We were on top of the world. Number one. We were Number one. Sometimes, for no reason at all, I just broke out laughing, I felt so good.

On television that night, I watched the replay of the game. Some people were already saying that if we played the Colts again on another day, the result would be different. I watched the game on TV and I saw how conservatively I'd played, how I went for field goals instead of touchdowns, and I guess I had to agree with those people.

On another day, we would have beat Baltimore worse.

**69**

# 3

I'd Rather
Play Football
than ... Almost
Anything

*I love football. I really love football. As far as I'm concerned, it's the second best thing in the world.*

We have a coach on the New York Jets named Walt Michaels, our defensive backfield coach, and for him, football is a life-and-death proposition. He bleeds every time our defense gives up a yard. He gets sick every time we get scored on. He gets high on victory. Well, I may not always look it, and I may not always sound it, but I'm the same way. I'm with Walt Michaels one hundred and ten percent.

*I honestly think I'd play football even if I didn't get paid for it. That sound you just heard in the background*

**73**

*was my lawyer and business adviser, Michael Bite, clutching his heart.*

I want to win every game I play. I want to play my best in every game. I like girls and I like Scotch, but I'd never do anything to hurt my own ability to play football or to hurt my team's chances of winning a game. Football means too damn much to me.

*Maybe if I played guard or tackle or linebacker, I woudn't love football so much. Those guys do all the hard work. I mean, they use up all their energy on the playing field. I like to save a little for afterward.*

It really pisses me off when people don't understand that I'm a football player first and anything else second, when they think that I'm just a playboy, just a swinger. Hell, I am a swinger, I do like to have a good time, but that's only one side of me, and I've got more than one side. There are a lot of guys just as good-looking as me—well, there are a few, anyway—who haven't made it in pro football. You can't make it just on good looks.

*I very rarely tackle and I almost never block. (Ever see me throw a block? I'm a regular matador; I wave my cape and step away.) I pass. And I could pass all day. I've figured out that in the past fifteen years I've thrown a minimum, an absolute minimum, of 250,000 passes. No matter what you've read in the gossip columns, there's nothing else in the world that I've done a quarter of a million times.*

You make it in pro football on talent, on conditioning, on practice and on study.

*I know I've got the talent. Vince Lombardi once called me a perfect passer. I wouldn't say that. But the man's been coaching for thirty years, and he ought to know what he's talking about.*

It's not easy for me to be serious for any length of time. I prefer a good laugh to a good lecture. But I am serious about football, and I'm serious about using my talent to the fullest. I stay in shape. Stop smiling. I know I'm not generally recognized as the world's leading author-ity on conditioning. I admit I don't always get nine hours of sleep a night, and I sometimes forget to drink six glasses of milk a day. But I've never been out of shape. I've never been overweight. I've never been too tired to play my best game of football.

My weight never falls below 195 and never goes above 205, and I try to keep myself trim. At the start of training camp each season, I do about fifty sit-ups at a time—hell, I can always do fifty, even in the middle of the off-season —and, gradually, I get up to two hundred at a time. I could do more. My middle stays flat. At least, I haven't heard any complaints yet from anybody who's had a good close-up look at it.

I don't do any running, none at all, because of my bad

**75**

knees, but my legs still get a lot of exercise, just from passing drills. Play after play, I'm dropping back seven yards
and throwing. I'm moving quickly, which is more important at my position than moving far. As long as I do
that sixty times a day at thirty-second intervals, I'm keeping my wheels in shape. I could run a mile and I wouldn't
equal what I'm getting there.

I laugh a lot in practice and I fool around with the other
guys, but I stop clowning when we go into our passing
drill. I love passing practice. I just enjoy the hell out of it.
I love throwing to Don Maynard and George Sauer and
Peter Lammons and Bake Turner and Bill Rademacher.
I love working on our timing, learning to anticipate every
move each man is going to make. These guys are beautiful
receivers, and every year we work together, every year
we get to know each other better, we become more effective. Timing is so damn important. Teamwork is so
damn important. You can have the greatest arm in the
world and you can throw the greatest pass, a lovely accurate bullet, but if the ball and the receiver don't end up
in the same place at the same time, you can cut off your
great arm for all the good it's doing you.

When I feel my timing's off, when I feel I need some
extra passing, I'll ask Maynard or Sauer or Lammons or
Rademacher or Turner to stay out after practice, and
they'll do it. They'll stay out on the field as long as I want
to throw. They enjoy catching passes just as much as I
enjoy throwing them.

I don't want to sound like I'm a big hero, killing myself
in practice every day. I'm not killing myself. I'm having

fun. Linemen kill themselves, but for me, all of football is fun, all of it except playing when I'm hurt. That's the only thing that I'd call work.

And I'm not saying that I put any more effort into my game than other quarterbacks put into theirs. All I'm saying is that, swinger or not, I'm just as interested in winning and practicing and training as anybody else. I've heard people say things like "Well, Namath's good, but if he had discipline, he'd be great." Goldang, I've got discipline. You've got to have discipline to be able to keep up with a schedule as busy as mine.

I spend plenty of time watching football and studying football. I don't watch football just because I'm supposed to. I watch football because I like football, because there's nothing else I'd rather watch. I watch games on television whenever I can, but usually we're playing when there's a game on, and Webb doesn't like me to bring my portable to the ballpark. Most of the time, I have to settle for watching movies. I put in an hour and a half or two hours a day at the stadium watching the films and discussing them with the coaches, analyzing our opponents, planning our offense. And I spend, on an average, about four or five hours a week at home watching football films, in prime time. I hear that Bart Starr of the Green Bay Packers spends ten or twenty hours a week watching movies at home, but Bart's got an advantage over me. He's married, and his wife takes care of the house. I'm a bachelor, and I have to waste a lot of time tidying up.

I deliberately haven't gotten very technical in explaining what we practice and what we look for in movies. I

**77**

could mention Q patterns and W patterns, flare patterns and fly patterns, look-ins and square-outs, but, hell, I'd probably just get everybody confused. I hear football fans talking sometimes in that special language they pick up and, shoot, I don't even know what they're talking about. They've got me doing things I never heard of.

I just want to tell you, as simply as possible, about one play, one play in which everything came together—conditioning, experience, practice, studying, everything—one play that sort of symbolized for me the whole 1968 season.

We were playing the Oakland Raiders for the championship of the American Football League. In the middle of the last quarter, they'd intercepted one of my passes and had gone on to score and were leading us, 23-20. We had to score.

I came out on the field after the kickoff, and we had the ball on our own thirty-two-yard line. I felt fresh. I felt strong. The adrenaline was flowing, and I felt confident that we would score.

*The personality of a quarterback is a very important thing. He has to believe in himself, and his teammates have to share his belief. My teammates pick up my confidence, just as I pick up theirs. For instance, when Winston Hill, our big tackle, says to me, "Joe, I can block that guy, I can get him," I know damn well he means it. There's no maybe, none of that "I think" stuff. On the field, it's too late to think; you've got to know.*

. . .

78

I threw one pass to Sauer, and we gained ten yards. I threw long to Maynard, and he made a great catch that carried us to the six-yard line of Oakland. It was first down and goal to go.

We went back in the huddle, and I knew exactly what I was going to do. I figured they'd be expecting a running play on first down, because we run a lot in first-and-goal situations. I figured they'd be expecting Matt Snell to carry the ball to the left side, because we'd used that play effectively against them before. I called for a fake to Snell, going into the left side, then a little pass out to the left to Bill Mathis, our other running back.

John Schmitt, our center, snapped the ball to me. The laces hit me in the right hand and, automatically, I had my grip.

*I mean, automatically. I can't even tell you where my hand goes on the ball without having a ball in front of me. I don't think about it at all. I just do it.*

I pivoted, carrying the ball low.

*On this particular play, faking to Snell, I had to keep the ball low. But I like to carry the ball low on every play. If I've got any little secret to my passing, that's it—carrying the ball low. Most quarterbacks carry the ball high, but I think that's ridiculous. I think that's a waste of time and energy. Right before you throw, you bring the ball down anyway, then bring it up, so I feel if I keep the ball low to start with, I'm saving one motion.*

**79**

. . .

I jammed the ball toward Snell's mid-section, then pulled it back and started to roll out to my left. Matt had blocked the linebacker on that side, but the linebacker had played it well, and he had me contained. I couldn't roll out the way I wanted to. I looked out to Mathis and raised the ball as though to pass it to him.

*I've got big hands, strong hands. They're not essential for a quarterback, but they sure help. I can palm a basketball so securely that I can actually wind up and pretend to throw and hold the ball back in one hand. When I was at the University of Alabama, every man on the football team had his grip tested, and I had the strongest grip. Any time I want, I can pump hard with a football, faking a pass, and still hold on to the ball.*

As I started to throw to Mathis, I saw that Dave Grayson, a defensive safety for Oakland, had come up and had Mathis covered. I held back the pass. I stumbled a bit. All the time, even as I was rolling out to pass to Mathis, even as the Oakland linemen were beginning to move in on me—hell, I don't even think about them; the worst they can do is kill me—I was looking to see how the rest of the Oakland defense was covering my receivers.

With Mathis covered, I looked for Sauer, who had been split out on the left and had gone straight downfield, then had cut to the center. I saw George was covered. Lammons, our tight end, had cut across from the right side to the left, and I saw that Pete was covered.

**80**

I was getting great blocking. I had five full seconds of protection.

Finally, I looked for Maynard.

*Three years earlier, two years earlier, maybe even a few months earlier, I wouldn't have had time to look for Don. I certainly wouldn't have had such strong blocking, and I wouldn't have been able to read the defense as quickly, to pick up the coverage on my receivers. This is the toughest part of the game for a quarterback, learning to read defenses, getting to know, almost by instinct, where his receivers are and where the defenders are.*

Maynard had started out on the right and had just sort of fooled around at the line of scrimmage, making a few moves, not going anywhere in particular, lulling the defender. When he saw that I was in trouble, that my primary and secondary receivers were covered, he broke down the middle. He was trying to outmaneuver George Atkinson, an Oakland rookie. It was Atkinson's interception that had set up Oakland's last touchdown. I'd tackled him after the interception—one of my rare tackles—on about our four-yard line. I knocked him out of bounds. As he got up, Atkinson said, "You sonovabitch, I hate you and I'm gonna kill you."

"Hey, man," I said. "Lighten up. Play the damn game right, man. Keep your mouth shut, you know."

*I don't hold any grudge against Atkinson for what he said. I separate what a man does on the field and what he's*

**81**

*like off the field. Maybe that's the way Atkinson works himself up for a game, getting himself to hate the quarterback. That's all right with me. I don't know Atkinson off the field, but he could be a helluva guy. I don't judge him by what he says in the heat of competition.*

The Raiders scored the play right after Atkinson intercepted. Hell, if I'd known they were going to do that, I wouldn't have even bothered tackling him.

Now, when I spotted Maynard working on Atkinson, I had to make an immediate decision. You can't throw if you think you've only got a fifty-fifty chance of getting the ball past the defender. Those aren't good enough odds. I was all ready to throw the ball away, to throw it over everybody's head and out of the end zone. But then I saw that Maynard had a step on Atkinson and I knew, instinctively, without measuring the pros and cons, that I could get the ball to him.

I decided to throw.

*I'm a natural passer. I mean, I throw the ball comfortably, easily, about three-quarters overhand most of the time, without putting any real strain on my arm. Many pro quarterbacks use an unnatural motion, and use it successfully, but it takes a lot out of their arms. Johnny U, for instance, when he throws, ends up with his wrist sort of twisted. That may be why he's been such a great passer over the years, but it may also be why his arm has bothered him so much in the last three or four years. I very rarely have a sore arm.*

**82**

*I started throwing a football twenty years ago, when I was six. My brother Bob, who was playing quarterback in junior high then, showed me how to grip the ball and, right from the beginning, he taught me not to wind up, but to throw from my ear. He taught me how to get rid of the ball fast; he taught me quick release, even though I'm sure neither of us had ever heard the expression then.*

*Later, when I was a sophomore in high school, one of the assistant coaches, a man named Leland Schackern, spent a lot of time with me. "Namath," he told me one afternoon, "I'm going to make a passer out of you." Mr. Schackern showed me how to throw the ball at different speeds and at different angles, how to loop one kind of pass and how to bullet another. While most kids my age were just hoping they could throw the ball the same way every time, I was varying my speed and my trajectory.*

Once I made the decision to try to hit Maynard, I knew I had to throw hard. I must have gone up a little more than three-quarters overhand, a little higher than usual, but still, just like my brother taught me, I threw from my ear. I threw the ball as hard as I've ever thrown a ball in my life. The ball zipped past Atkinson and found Maynard in the end zone. He caught it and fell to his knees and we had a touchdown, and after Jim Turner kicked the extra point, we were winning, 27-23.

We won the game, 27-23. We won the championship of the American Football League. When the game ended, Cornell Gordon, one of our defensive backs, and I just started hugging and slapping each other right on the field.

**83**

"We did it, we did it, we did it," we both kept saying. We were laughing and shouting and, actually, crying. I cried, I felt so good.

Winning is what the game is all about. Anytime we win a game, I don't really care what my own personal performance was. I don't care if I threw five touchdown passes or none, if I completed twenty passes or two. I don't give a damn as long as we win.

But, I'll tell you, I just felt perfect after that Oakland game. I was really worried about Oakland, more than I was about Baltimore in the Super Bowl, and I just about exploded inside when we won that game. It couldn't have happened any better way, the combination of winning plus throwing a touchdown pass to win the game.

It's pretty hard to describe how that feels, throwing a pass and seeing a man catch it and seeing him in the end zone and seeing the referee throw his arms up in the air, signaling a touchdown, signaling that you've done just what you set out to do. It's an incredible feeling. It's like your whole body's bursting with happiness.

*I guess there's only one thing in the world that compares with it.*

# 4

## I Like
## My Girls Blond
## and My
## Johnnie Walker Red

I have pretty good will power. On April 12, 1967, to win a bet, I stopped smoking cigarettes. I'll never smoke another.

If a doctor told me I had to give up drinking, I'm sure I could give it up tomorrow.

If a doctor told me I had to give up women, I'm sure I'd give up doctors.

My will power has limits.

Women are the best thing going in the world. I've got nothing against guys. They're great to drink with and to play cards with and to laugh with, and I like to have them blocking for me on the football field.

But, if I have to, I can go a week or two or even three

**87**

without seeing a guy. I don't want to go a day without seeing a woman.

I like women. I prefer tall blondes but, shoot, I really like them all, tall, short, experienced, innocent, amateurs, pros, blondes, brunettes, just about everything there is, except redheads. I don't know what it is, but redheads don't turn me on. It's got to be my fault, not theirs. I guess I just haven't met the right redheads yet.

I have my own golden rule that I apply to women: Make her happy, and she'll make you happy; look after her, and she'll look after you. I really believe that. Hell, it's got to be a two-way street. I know some guys who look at women just like objects, just like something they can use, and I think that's plain sick. Women are just too good to be treated like that.

I've got respect for women, all kinds of women. There are some girls I meet who I know are not going to be easy. I mean, sometimes I'm a genuine eighteen-point underdog. They like me and they like my company, but they don't want a guided tour of my apartment. I can understand that. Well, no, I can't really understand it. I can't imagine any-one who doesn't enjoy sex, who doesn't want sex all the time. It's the best thing ever invented. But if I meet a girl and I like her, and she's just interested in conversation, well, hell, I can still enjoy being with her. And, sometimes, it turns out that the point spread was wrong, that I should have been a favorite all along. I remember one chick who was just so cool, proper and poised and everything, a tall Southern belle. Goldang, she almost killed me later on. I thought Ben Davidson, that Oakland end who broke my

**88**

jaw, had caught up to me again. She was damn near as big as Davidson. The only way I knew it wasn't Davidson was that she didn't have a mustache.

You never know how an evening's going to turn out. Once I was in Las Vegas, and some guy put a hooker on me, like a present or something. She owed him some favors. We had a few drinks and went up to my room, and we started talking, and it turned out she was from Freedom, Pennsylvania, just a few miles from my hometown. I thought that was funny as hell, going all the way to Las Vegas to find a prostitute from home. She was a nice girl—I mean, she knew her business, but she was still a nice girl—and I don't put her down at all for her line of work. All I know is that she was good to me, and that's how I judge people. We talked for hours, about football—where I come from, even the hookers are football fans—and about her game. I was really interested in what she had to say. I wanted to know what it was like for her to be with a seventy-year-old guy, whether she could do him any good, things like that. Hell, I'm going to be seventy myself someday.

I don't want to give the impression that I consider myself an expert on sex. I suppose I know a little more about that than I know about political science, but I'm no professional. I'm just an avid amateur. I came to the game late. I'd been throwing a football for ten years before I learned about other kinds of fun.

I discovered sex when I was sixteen years old, a sophomore in high school. One of my friends and I went to visit a girl at her home. She was an older woman as far as we

**89**

were concerned, a high school senior, eighteen. She told my friend to wait downstairs while she took me upstairs. I thought she just wanted me to see her house. When I found out she had other ideas, I wasn't scared. I just didn't know what the hell to do. I'd played doctor a few times, but that was about it; I'd never gotten into the operating room.

We went into her bedroom and we didn't even get undressed. It was just like lifting up her skirt and—surprise! It was kind of funny, and kind of nice. I don't get many surprises any more. I guess I wasn't too considerate of her; I didn't know what I was doing. She probably doesn't even remember any of it—it sure as hell wasn't her first time—but I remember it. I remember all of them. I even remember most of the names.

(One night early in 1969, I was sitting in Bachelors III, and a girl came in and kept staring at me. I didn't know who the hell she was. Finally, she walked over to me and said, "Hi." I said, "Hi," too. "You don't remember me, do you?" she said. Right there, it hit me. "Barbara," I said, "how can you say that? How dare you think I'd forget you?" I'll tell you, once I did remember her name, I don't know how I ever forgot her. What a crazy broad! I was in her car with her once, and she was pulling out of a garage, and she crashed into a pillar, pulled over to the other side and hit a wall, backed up and just drove right out, without a word. How could I forget Barbara?)

About a year or two after my introduction to sex, I remember I was in the back seat of a car with a girl, and something good was happening, and all of a sudden, at the worst possible moment, I got a goldang cramp in my leg.

**90**

That was the first time my legs betrayed me.

That was also the last time I tried to make love in a car. I learned a lesson.

I'm still learning. I'm fortunate that I've met a lot of good teachers. I don't date much—I mean, I don't take girls to dinner or to the theater or to the movies very often—but I like to go out at night and just see what I bump into. I'm lucky, I suppose. I bump into a lot of good things. Maybe it's the kind of life I lead. I fly a lot, and I'm kind of nervous in planes, so I like to talk to the stewardesses. If they make me feel good in the air, I like to do the same for them on the ground. During the off-season, I live in Miami and, by a coincidence, the Playboy Club of Miami is right across the street from my barber. Some people say I don't go to the barber often enough, but I sure do get into his neighborhood a lot. When I'm in New York, I've got a field of about four million females to choose from, and most of the best ones seem to live in my neighborhood, the swinging East Side. I believe in being a good neighbor.

I guess some of the girls I bump into in New York would like to see my apartment—they've heard and read so much about it—and I don't like to disappoint them. Some of them seem disappointed, anyway, when they find out that my famous llama-skin rug has been cut up into little pieces. That's the only thing they want to see, the llama-skin rug. I guess the big mirror on the ceiling of the bedroom just isn't as interesting. But I do have an antique Spanish galleon that's kind of exciting.

I don't want you to think I go running after girls all the time. Once in a while, they come running after me. There

**91**

seem to be girls all over the United States who have nothing better to do than write me letters and tell me how much they enjoy watching me play football. Some of them send their pictures, and some of the pictures are pretty wild. I mean, hell, I like to have a little left to my imagination. Most of the girls just want my autograph or my picture, but a few of them want something more personal.

Take a letter I got a few months after the Super Bowl game:

> Dear Joe,
>
> I know you probably won't remember me, but we met at a fraternity party at the University of Alabama. We didn't meet for long, but I thought I'd write to ask you to give me a call when you come back to Alabama . . .
>
> If you can't place my face with my name, just let me know and I'll drop a photo in the mail to refresh your memory.

Now, that sounds like a perfectly innocent letter, right? There was just one thing in it that made me a little suspicious. You know where she said, "I thought I'd write to ask you to give me a call when you come back to Alabama . . ."? Well, in the word "call," she had written the letter *c* over the letter *b*. Now, maybe, her pen had just slipped, but it sure slipped at a funny spot. And there were no other letters written over in the whole note. I'll tell you, I get a letter like that, and it kind of scares me. I don't think she's going to be too happy if I just send her an autographed picture of me in my New York Jets uniform.

I may be misjudging the girl. I have misjudged girls before. One time it was kind of embarrassing. My first year in New York, I hung out a lot in a spot called Dudes and Dolls. It was a good place, a swinging place, and I got to know several of the girls who worked there as dancers and as waitresses. I was in there one night, sitting at a table, and they had a go-go dancer working, a real big girl, and she looked pretty good to me. I thought I might make a move. I turned to one of the waitresses I knew and I said, "Boy, she doesn't look too bad."

"Leave her alone, Joe," the waitress said.

"I wouldn't mind getting to know her," I said.

"Joe, forget it," the waitress said. "Joe, she's not a girl."

"What do you mean, she's not a girl?" I said. "Don't bullshit me."

"Look close, Joe."

I looked close and, damn, if that waitress wasn't right. It was a guy dressed up and made up like a girl. You could tell when you looked real hard at her—his—features. She —he—had big bones, a square chin, muscular legs. Shoot, he was a big mother. I almost made a rash decision that night. I almost gave up drinking.

I did give up drinking at one point during the 1968 season, and it wasn't because of any go-go dancer. It was all Jim Hudson's fault. Jim and I are roommates on the road, and we're pretty tight. I go over to his house every now and then to eat dinner; his wife makes good Southern food and Mexican food. After we won our first two games of the season, we were getting ready to play Buffalo, and Hud and I were driving back to Manhattan together after our Tuesday practice.

"Joe," Hud said, "I got a helluva idea."

"Good," I said. I looked away from him.

"You want to hear it?" he said.

"No, I don't want to hear it," I said, "but if you want to tell it, I'll listen."

"I think we ought to stop drinking," Hud said.

"What?"

"I think we ought to stop drinking. We're just drinking too damn much."

I knew Jim was starting to think seriously that we could win the American Football League championship. I thought I'd humor him a little. "Shit, Jim," I said, "we'll cut down a little bit."

"Well, I didn't feel good out there at practice today," Jim said. "I think we just better stop."

"I'll tell you what," I said. "You stop and I'll cut down."

"Oh, no, we got to do it together."

"Here's what we'll do, then," I said. "We'll stop drinking Scotch and we'll drink wine."

"Hell, that's not quitting," Hud said. "Let's just quit this week and we'll see what it does. We'll see how we feel."

I gave in. "Oh, hell, all right," I said.

We went four and a half days without a drink, and on Sunday, we were favored by nineteen points over Buffalo. The Bills hadn't won a game. That was the day I threw those five interceptions, and Buffalo beat us.

"Damn you, Hudson," I said in the locker room, after the game. "It's your fault. Don't you ever talk to me about not drinking again."

I started drinking again that night and I drank right

through the following Sunday, when I threw no interceptions and we whipped San Diego.

Then, a day or two later, I came down with the flu, and I was sick in bed and I was taking medication and I wasn't able to drink almost the whole week. On Sunday, we played Denver, and again we were favored by nineteen points. I threw five more interceptions, and Denver beat us.

I don't know what would have happened to the Jets if I hadn't been able to start drinking again that night. I don't know what would have happened to Johnnie Walker. I drank the whole rest of the season and I had a total of only five passes intercepted in the next nine games. I was relaxed. I wasn't tight. I could throw good.

It was probably just a coincidence, my not drinking and my throwing all those interceptions, but after the Denver defeat my teammates didn't want to take any chances. "Just leave him alone," they kept telling Hudson. "Just let him do what he wants." They may even have chipped in and sent me a few cases.

Then, when we were preparing to play Oakland for the title, I was in the sauna bath one day and I was starting to get excited about the game. "C'mon, now," I was telling everybody. "We got to be up for this game. We got to play our best. We really got to take care of ourselves. I think I'll even stop drinking."

Well, about six of the guys just pounced on me right in the sauna. Dave Herman, a big offensive guard and tackle, grabbed me and said, "Don't you start that stop-drinking shit, Joe. Damn you, don't you dare stop drinking. I'll kill you."

**95**

I'm afraid of Dave. He's a tough boy. But I disobeyed him. I stopped drinking—twelve hours before the kickoff.

Don't get the wrong idea. I'm not an alcoholic. I only drink on two occasions, when I'm with people and when I'm alone. I came to drinking late, just like I came to girls late, and maybe that's why I appreciate both of them so much. In high school, I only drank wine. In college, I began to enjoy beer, but during the season I hardly ever snuck a drink. It wasn't until I turned pro that I moved up in class, that I began sipping Johnnie Walker Red. I drink for the same reason I keep company with girls. It makes me feel good. It takes away the tension. Once the tension's gone, I don't keep on drinking. I don't go to bed completely bombed. I don't want to wake up with an aching head. That's bad for you.

I can only remember one time when I really got bombed the night before a game. It was the last game of my second season in New York. We were playing the Boston Patriots, and the game didn't mean anything to us as far as the standings were concerned. We went into the game with a record of five victories, six defeats and two ties. If we won, we finished third in the Eastern Division, and if we lost, we finished third in the Eastern Division. But the game meant the whole season to Boston. If they won, they were the champions of the Eastern Division; if they lost, they were in second place.

The night before the game was incredible, just unbelievable. I was in a club about 1:30, 2 A.M., minding my own business, just getting a nightcap before going to sleep, and I got a phone call that some guy was coming to get me with a knife. That made me a little nervous, so I had to have a few more drinks to steady myself. The guy never showed up, of course—it was just some wild threat—but I really quenched my thirst waiting for him.

When I showed up at the stadium for the game, I was whacked out. I was gone. I was holding onto things to keep from falling down while I was getting taped. My head was just pounding something awful.

I wasn't too anxious to play football, but I didn't think Weeb would accept my excuse. I played. I threw twenty-one passes and completed fourteen of them, three for touchdowns, for a total of 287 yards. We beat the Patriots, 38-28. To this day, I don't know what happened during that game. It was the last game of the year, so I didn't see the films, and I just don't know what happened. I guess my receivers must have had a helluva day.

Even though I've got a perfect record—one for one—in games played while whacked out of my head, I don't recommend it. I drink light the night before a game, just enough to get myself loose. But I don't see any reason why I can't get a little mellow the rest of the week, not blind-drunk or anything stupid like that, just happy. Except for that one game, that Boston game, I've always been ready to play on Sunday. My head's always been clear, my body's always felt good and my attitude's always been beautiful. I think my teammates understand—hell, outside of Johnny Sample and Paul Crane, most of them drink, too—and they know I'm not going to let them down. I think my coaches understand, too. They didn't always understand.

During my second season, we played a game out in

**97**

Denver, and for some reason, we went out there a few days early. Maybe Weeb wanted us to get adjusted to the altitude or something. We left New York at a terrible hour, like six thirty or seven one morning, and I remember I was in bad shape. My head hurt too much for me to get all dressed up for the flight, so I just put on a pair of Bermudas, a pair of slippers and a Ban-Lon shirt, stuck my toothbrush in my pocket and got on the plane. When we reached Denver, I picked up the rest of the things I needed.

If I remember right, we got there on Thursday and we were playing on Sunday, and Weeb put in a ten-thirty curfew. Who the hell goes to sleep at ten thirty? Well, Thursday night, I went out with one of the Denver ballplayers—he knew the good spots—and after we had a few drinks and met a few girls and danced a little, I asked him, "What time is it?"

"It's ten thirty," he said.

"I'm having too much fun," I said. "Shoot, I'm not going in yet."

About eleven thirty or twelve, Bill Hampton, our equipment manager, came into the club where I was relaxing. "Hey, Bill, Billy," I said. "What are you doing here? I didn't expect to see you here."

I was really glad to see him. Bill's a helluva guy. He had to be a helluva guy to find me. "Joe, c'mon," he said. "The coach sent me out here to get you. You gotta come in now."

"Billy," I said, "Billy, settle down. Settle down right here at the bar."

"C'mon, Joe. We got to go."

**98**

"Give me a Scotch," I told the bartender, "and give him a Scotch."

"No, Joe, no."

"You got to take care of me, Billy," I said. "You can't let me drink alone. That wouldn't be right."

He was supposed to get me to stop drinking, but instead I got him started. Bill's not much of a drinker, and after a couple he was pretty high and he was worried to death. "Joe, Joe, what am I going to do?" he kept saying. "I was sent out here to get you. What am I going to do?"

"Hell, don't worry about it, Bill," I said. "You did your best. You tried. You couldn't get me to come in, that's all. I'll tell Weeb you tried. Don't worry about a thing."

Around 1 A.M., the bartender told me there was a phone call for me. I thought it might be something interesting, but it was just Chuck Knox, one of our assistant coaches.

"Hello, Joe," he said. "Joe, this is Chuck. Joe, it's after curfew."

"Ah, Chuck, right, sorry about that," I said. "Gee, I'm sorry about that."

"You come back now, Joe," he said.

"Ah, Chuck, do I have to?"

"You better. You better come back."

I was thinking perfectly clearly. "It's one o'clock now, right?" I told Chuck. "If I come in now, I'm going to get fined four hundred dollars, five hundred dollars, right? If I come in at nine or ten in the morning, I'm going to get fined four hundred dollars, five hundred dollars. So what the hell should I be coming in now for?"

**99**

I thought my logic was pretty good, but Chuck argued with me. "Joe, you got a game coming up," he said.

"I know," I said. "That's not till Sunday."

"Joe, I'm just trying to help you," said Chuck.

"Right, right, Chuck," I said. "Why don't you come out here and we'll talk about it?"

"I don't think Weeb would like that. Really, Joe, why don't you come in?"

"Well, really, Chuck, I don't think I should."

He gave up. "Well, Joe," he said, "you do what you think is best."

I got back to the hotel in another hour or two, long before daylight. I paid my fine. I got four or five hours of sleep before practice. And we beat Denver on Sunday.

One of the things that makes Weeb Ewbank such a great coach is that we don't practice in the mornings. My first year or two, I thought we ought to practice in the morning so that we could get it out of the way and have the rest of the day free to do whatever we wanted. But Weeb feels it's a good idea to practice at the same hour you play your games, and I've got to say now that the man is absolutely right.

We practiced just once in the morning in 1968, Thanksgiving morning, and that one session made a believer out of me. We were going to have a big team luncheon, all the players and their wives and children, so Weeb called a morning practice. It was the worst thing you ever saw. It was beyond belief. I couldn't throw the ball. I couldn't hit a receiver from five yards away. I couldn't function properly. I was lucky I was able to lift my arm. Hell, if the Colts had played us in the morning, they might have won the Super Bowl.

The whole explanation to my swinging image—well, part of the explanation, anyway—is that I've got a strange schedule. I get up around eleven o'clock each day and I spend the afternoon practicing and watching game movies. I relax in the evening, maybe look at films and write a few letters and eat dinner and take a nap. And then I go out. I go out from eleven to three. If we had a different practice schedule, I'd probably get up at eight each day, work in the morning, relax in the afternoon and then go out at night from eight to twelve. Then nobody would think I'm so wild. Then I'd just be keeping the same schedule as most people.

What I'm trying to say is that I'm really just a normal guy who happens to be on an abnormal schedule.

Someday I'm going to settle down. Someday I'm going to cut out the night life. Someday I'm going to get married.

I've even got a girl in mind, a girl I think I could spend the rest of my life with. Her name is Suzie Storm—you've got to admit that's a helluva name—and she's the most wonderful girl I've ever met. Suzie's tall and blond and beautiful, and she's real. I just like being with her. I'm relaxed with her. I feel good.

Suzie just finished college in Pensacola, Florida. She sang with a rock group in college, and she majored in French. She's a bright girl. When Suzie comes to New York, we go places like the Museum of Modern Art and, damn, I enjoy it. I enjoy being anywhere with Suzie.

But I'm not going to get married yet, not for another

couple of years, anyway. The kind of life I lead, I know that if I got married right now, I wouldn't be a good husband. I'd cheat. There are just too many opportunities, and I'm human.

I've seen too many guys my age, leading my kind of life, who cheat in their marriages. I can't condemn them because, hell, I've never been married. I don't know what it's like. Maybe you can run around and still love your wife, I don't know. But when I get married, I'm going to try to stick to one woman. I hope I'll be able to. I hope I won't have missed much by then.

And I hope Suzie's patient. She's been patient so far. She's put up with me, and I know that's not easy. She deserves a medal.

The lady is a saint.

# 5

They Probably
Would've
Told Our Lord
to Cut His Hair

> "This above all—to thine own self be true,
> And it must follow, as the night the day,
> Thou canst not then be false to any man."
> —SHAKESPEARE

That's the kind of things I've got to put up with when I hang around writers. The way I heard it was: Do your own thing.

I was in the police station in Miami in the spring of 1969, and I wasn't signing autographs. I'd been arrested for reckless driving, and I'd taken a drunkometer test and I'd passed it, and I was waiting for my lawyer. A couple of cops came in, escorting three young people, two guys and a girl. The cops put the girl in one cell and the two guys in another cell with a young black kid.

I wondered what they had done. I walked over to one of the cops. "Sir," I said, "why did you bring these people in?"

"Brought them in on vagrancy," he said.

**105**

"Why?" I said.

"They didn't have any jobs," he said. "They didn't have any place to go. They were just sitting in their car."

"Maybe that's their thing," I said. "Maybe that's what they want to do. They weren't bothering anybody, were they?"

"They were parked on property they shouldn't have been on," the cop said.

"What kind of property?" I said.

"Private property. They were parked in their car there, and they were all sleeping. They're vagrants."

"Did you ask them to move, sir?"

"They were breaking the law," the cop said. "We brought them in 'cause they were breaking the law. My job's to enforce the law, not to interpret it."

"Maybe they just wanted to rest," I said.

"Nah," he said. "They're filthy kids. They don't bathe, and they got long hair. One of them's got a beard."

I had a goatee myself, and my hair wasn't exactly crew-cut. I think I said something unkind to the cop. He didn't smile. I walked away from him and walked over to the cell with the three guys.

"Hey, what's happening?" I said. "You all right?"

Another cop came marching up to me. "Get away from there," he said. "You can't talk to them."

"Why not?" I said. "I'm just passing the time. I'm not hurting anybody. They're not hurting anybody."

"You want to talk to them," the cop said, "you get in that cell with them. I'll lock you up in there, too."

Well, hell, I figured the company in there was better than

**106**

the company I had outside the cell. "Shit, man," I said, "if that's the way you feel, lock me up."

He opened the cell, and I went in, and he locked the door, and I sat down on the floor and started rapping with the kids.

They were good kids. They hadn't washed in a while—the cop was right about that—but that's no reason to put them in jail. One of the kids had the best manners I ever saw. He was so polite. He just seemed like a helluva kid. We had a good time talking.

Those kids were doing their thing, and they weren't causing anybody any trouble. I didn't think they should be in jail. It really pissed me off. Hell, they're my people, the young people, the "now" people. I dig the music—Aretha Franklin, Janis Joplin, Tom Jones, The Fifth Dimension, Bobbie Gentry, Burt Bacharach, all of it, all kinds of music—and I dig the clothes and I dig most of all the feeling, the freedom, the idea of live-and-let-live.

If I've got to try to put everything I feel into one sentence, it's this: *I think anybody should be allowed to do anything he wants to do as long as he doesn't hurt himself or anyone else.*

That's not a terribly profound thought, and it's not very complicated. But not everybody agrees with me I've discovered from reading my mail:

Sir:

Get a haircut, you bum! Millions of young men want to be like you. If you act like a bum, they want to act like a bum. If you wear your hair like a girl, they want to wear their hair like a girl.

**107**

Wake up! Do something for your country. Maybe you're 4-F, but at least you can get a clean-cut image and quit breaking speeding laws.

If you reform, the kids will follow you.

It's nice to get fan mail. I mean, it's good therapy for those people in institutions to be allowed to write letters.

Actually, that's one of the more polite letters I received. The fellow forgot to accuse me of rape, murder or jaywalking, like some of the people do.

Those people have got to be insane. In the first place, I get my hair cut fairly often. I want it to look right. I want the sideburns to come down to the right spot, and I want it all to look neat. In the second place, I don't know any girls who wear their hair the way I wear mine. If they want to, fine, but most of the girls I know prefer something a little more feminine. And anybody who can't tell the difference between my hair and a girl's hair is liable to get himself in a lot of trouble someday.

Most important, what the hell difference does it make how I wear my hair? Suppose it hangs down to my toes. Who does it hurt, except me, when I'm trying to get away from a tackler?

The Only Perfect Man who ever lived had a beard and long hair and didn't wear shoes and slept in barns and didn't hold a regular job and never put on a tie. I'm not comparing myself with Him—I'm in enough trouble trying to stack up against Bart Starr—but I'm just saying that you don't judge a man by the way he cuts his hair. Shoot, I never saw a picture of a saint who didn't have long hair. Abraham Lincoln had a beard, and George Washington wore a wig. Sure, I know there've been famous people who were clean-cut, too, like John Dillinger, for instance.

I don't get angry too often, but sometimes something just bugs the hell out of me. A few months after the Super Bowl, I saw a story in a Miami newspaper about a coach kicking a boy off the high school baseball team because he had long sideburns. The coach said he didn't want any dirty people on his team. He said athletes are supposed to be clean-cut and people with long hair and sideburns are not clean people. I almost called that idiot on the phone. That coach could be ruining a boy's life over something he has no right to judge. If the boy wants to wear sideburns, that's his business. To say that he's not a clean person because he wears sideburns is worse than ridiculous.

I had something happen to me that got me almost as angry. I like to play golf. I can't play as much as I'd like to because of my legs, but still, during the off-season, I play twenty or thirty times. In Miami, once a week or once every two weeks, I play at La Gorce Country Club, which is really a beautiful course. It's a private club, and I know a lot of the members, and I can play there almost anytime I like. I don't play there too often because J don't like to impose. I don't like to be somebody's guest all the time.

In 1968 one of my friends who was on the board of directors at La Gorce asked me if I'd like to be proposed for membership. I said sure, I'd like to belong to La Gorce.

"I'll check into it," my friend said.

A few days later, he called me up and told me that my chances didn't look too good, that if I cleaned myself up and cut my hair, I might have a shot at it. I kind of forgot the whole thing.

Then, in early 1969, my friend spoke to me again about joining La Gorce. "I'll sponsor you," he said.

A week or two later, he phoned me. "It's all set, Joe," he said. "You can join, if you'll just do one thing."

"What's that?" I said.

"Just shave your beard," he said.

He's a nice man, and I like him, and I suppose I shouldn't have told him exactly what he could do with La Gorce Country Club. I mean, it's a short course, but it's not *that* short.

If I'm going to join a country club, or a Rotary Club, or a Touchdown Club, or anything, they'll just have to take me the way I am. I'm the same guy when I'm totally shaven and when I've got a Fu Manchu mustache; the only difference is a few ounces of weight.

I like having a goatee. I even grew one when I was in high school. I grew another one when I was in college, after my junior season. And I've grown the goatee three or four different times since I joined the New York Jets.

The goatee alone never got as much publicity as the Fu Manchu mustache I sprouted during the 1968 season. I guess a million people must know I got $10,000 for shaving it off for a razor commercial. But what most of the people don't know is that I decided to shave it before I got the commercial, not the other way around. I woke up one morning and I just felt like shaving. So I called up Jimmy Walsh, my lawyer in New York, and said, "Jimmy, I'm ready to shave. See if you can get a commercial." And he did.

I don't mean to dwell too much on beards and sideburns

**110**

and long hair, but I guess they're sort of a symbol of the way I feel about things, and of the way some people feel about me. I'm not a psychiatrist, I can't explain it, but I think there's something strange about people picking on my hair. I can't believe that it's really the way I wear my hair that upsets them. It's got to be something else, some hangup they've got, so they talk about my hair.

I don't like people telling me what to do. I don't like people telling me how to act or who to be friendly with. I don't go around telling anybody else what to do. I respect a man's own ideas, his own style. I've got a teammate named Paul Crane, who went to the University of Alabama with me, and Paul doesn't drink or smoke or swear. When I'm around Paul, I try not to swear, because I know it hurts him. In fact, I made a bet with him that I'd give him fifty cents every time I swore in front of him on the field. I cut down my swearing quite a bit. Every time I'd say, "Mother," I'd look up and see Paul and not finish the word. Most of the time, except in front of ladies, I do swear a lot. I don't mean anything by using cuss words; maybe I just don't have a good enough vocabulary.

I hate to do anything against my own will, against my own values, no matter how practical it seems. (Sometimes, you have to conform; like, if I want to go to "21" for dinner, I wear a tie. Nobody forces me to go to "21," but I like the place and I know if I want to go there I've got to wear a tie.) Before the battle over Bachelors III, before I agreed to sell the club, I can think of only one time I did something I really didn't want to do.

At the University of Alabama, the athletes have an

**111**

organization called A Club. If you win a letter, you're eligible for membership (and unless you join, you can't wear your letter). Well, I won my football letter in the fall of my sophomore year, and I was invited to join A Club. I said no. I didn't want to join. For initiation, they shave you bald and beat you with a paddle and and make you do asinine things like drinking Tabasco sauce. I wasn't going to do it. I didn't see any sense to it.

Ray Abruzzese, my roommate now, had been a senior at Alabama when I was a freshman, and he'd been the guy I was closest to, the guy who helped me the most. Ray hadn't joined A Club, and I didn't think I had to.

One afternoon, Paul Bryant, my football coach, called me to his office. "Joe," he said. "Let's take a ride. I want to talk to you."

We got in his car and went for a drive. "Joe," said Coach Bryant, "I understand you're not going through A Club initiation."

"Yes, sir," I said. "That's right."

"Why is that, boy?"

"I don't believe in it, sir," I said. "I don't believe in shaving my hair and that stuff. I earned my letter and I think I should be able to wear it without going through that stuff."

"Well," Coach Bryant said, "you know it's tradition here at the school."

"I don't go for that tradition," I said.

"You know, Joe," Coach Bryant said, "you can't ever be a captain of the team if you don't go through A Club."

I almost laughed. Big deal. Who the hell wants to be a captain? "Coach," I said, "I don't care about that."

"Well, Joe," he said, "I'd like for you to go through it. I want you to go through it."

I did it. I couldn't say no to Coach Bryant. I guess it was a combination of respect and fear, and maybe I didn't feel too strongly about not joining A Club. After I became a member, though, I didn't participate in initiation ceremonies for other guys. I didn't believe in it.

I'm still a little sorry I joined A Club; it went against my principles. But there aren't many things I've done in my life that I'm sorry for. Most of the time, I just enjoy myself. I really enjoy myself. I love my life, and I don't think I'd trade places with anyone. I'd trade knees with just about anybody, but not places.

The thing I like best about my life is that I can do almost whatever I want to do. I don't have to conform to anybody else's standards. Take the way I dress. I think I dress pretty well—I'm up-to-date, I'm mod—and I don't really care too much what anybody else thinks. Some people got really shook up when I posed in that $5,000 fur coat. Hell, I didn't go out and buy the coat; I got it free for posing for the picture. It's not the sort of thing I'd go out and buy— I just don't have any need for a fur coat—but I don't think there's anything wrong with it. The coat was stolen during the week of the Super Bowl, but I might get another one, as long as I just have to pose for a picture for it.

I don't spend a lot of money on my clothes, and I don't go on too many shopping sprees. If I feel like I need a suit, I get one. If I feel like I need slacks, I get a pair. I dress for my own comfort more than anything else. For instance, I can't wear anything next to my skin that's woolly or coarse; it just itches the hell out of me.

**113**

I've got plenty of sports clothes and I've got plenty of suits, smart three-button suits. I always button the top two buttons on my suits; I think that looks best on me. When I first moved to New York, I think I had maybe one suit to my name. I never wore suits in college, except on very special occasions. My first season with the Jets, I went to see *Funny Girl* on Broadway, and I wore a sports shirt and a sports jacket—and posed for photos like that with Barbra Streisand—and I was actually surprised when Mr. Werblin—David A. Werblin, who was then the president of the Jets—bawled me out for the way I dressed. I just didn't know any better.

I know better now. I wear suits to the places where you're supposed to wear suits, or else I don't go there. Most nights in New York, I go to informal spots, and I can dress any way I like, a suit or slacks and a sports shirt. In the off-season, in Miami, most of the time during the day, I wear a sports shirt and either Bermudas or hip-huggers. Incidentally, in the spring of 1969, my friend at La Gorce told me I could join now without shaving my beard. All I had to do was dress a little neater. I still don't belong.

For recreation, I do my own thing. Hell, I like talking to my friends as well as almost anything. Three or four of them are always stopping by my apartment. Maybe we'll go over to the Copa and catch an act we enjoy, or maybe we'll run over to Mr. Laff's, the spot owned by Bobby Anderson, a former football player, and Phil Linz, a former baseball player, and check the action there, or maybe we'll just sit up in the apartment, sipping Scotch and watching television. I can have fun in little ways. I

**114**

remember once, on a sunny fall afternoon in New York, I bought a big bunch of flowers and walked down the street handing them out to each woman I met. I smiled, and they smiled, and it was beautiful.

I've gone to the theater in New York only five times—*Funny Girl, Oh! Calcutta!, Golden Boy, King Lear* and *Hair*—and you'd never guess which one I liked best. I loved *King Lear*. I'm not too hip on Shakespeare, but that Lee J. Cobb was terrific. I went just to keep a friend company, but I really liked it. The show I liked least was *Hair*. You know, I couldn't stand all those people with long hair and sideburns. No, that wasn't why I didn't like it. It just didn't turn me on. I thought it was a dirty show. I know that sounds funny coming from me but, hell, I'm not always easy to figure out. I have trouble myself sometimes.

I don't like to go to too many public places, like theaters or restaurants, because it can turn into a mob scene. (No, I don't mean *that* mob.) I don't mind people asking me for my autograph. Well, I do mind sometimes, when I'm in a hurry or when it drags on for a long time, with hundreds of people lined up, but most of the time I enjoy it. I enjoy the attention. I'm glad some people think I'm a hero, not a bum. I've got my heroes, too—Bill Hartack, Sammy Davis Jr., Nureyev, Sinatra, anybody who can do something really fantastically well—and, hell, I like knowing that some people think I'm special. I dig people, and if they like me, that's great. If they don't like me, that's okay, too. I just wish the people who don't like me would stop asking me for autographs. I mean, that's real hypocrisy.

**115**

Generally, I'm nice to people, but once in a while I slip.

Early in 1969, I was going to New York to make an appearance at the annual sportsman's show. I stopped in Pensacola to pick up Suzie Storm, and then we caught a flight to New Orleans. Our plane got delayed, and we reached New Orleans two or three hours late, and we had to run to try to catch a flight leaving for New York. We ran just about the length of the airport and found out that the flight was going to take off an hour and a half late. I was really upset. I knew I wasn't going to get to the show on time.

Suzie and I decided to get something to eat at the airport restaurant, and while we were walking through the terminal, a pack of about twenty kids recognized me and stopped me for my autograph. That wasn't too bad.

Then we got into the restaurant, and while we were ordering our meal, maybe half a dozen people came over for autographs. I signed for all of them.

Then my food arrived, and I was hungry. I had my fork in my hand, ready to dig in, and a guy walked over and put his arm around me and said, "Excuse me, Joe, can I interrupt you?"

"Hell, no," I said. "I'm eating."

The guy was embarrassed. He sort of straightened up and walked away, and when I saw him leave the restaurant with another man and with a lady, I could tell he was really hurt. I'd let myself get upset, and I'd upset him.

The whole rest of the day, I thought about that man. The man hadn't done anything to me, and I'd hurt him. It was a long day for me, a bad day.

# 6

# There Are No Coal Mines in Beaver Falls

I was going home, back to Beaver Falls on May 24, 1969, to celebrate the first, and possibly last, "Joe Namath Day." I don't think it'll ever be a national holiday. I had just a small group with me—a lawyer, a public-relations man, a television crew, half a dozen photographers and writers, a couple of teammates, a few friends and two tension-easers, a tall one and a short one. You can't go home empty-handed.

The short one was wearing a completely transparent blouse. When our plane from New York landed in Pittsburgh, some guy from a local newspaper rushed up to the young lady and said, "Excuse me, miss, but is that a see-through blouse?"

I realize that most reporters are half-blind, anyway, but this guy was ridiculous. I mean, if he couldn't tell that was a see-through blouse, what did he think they were?

She answered his question very frankly, and after the guy recovered, we all piled into limousines for the twenty-eight-mile trip to Beaver Falls. I was a little nervous. Not for myself; I knew I'd survive. For Beaver Falls.

*I arrived in Beaver Falls for the first time, May 31, 1943, a big disappointment to my parents, Rose and John Namath. They'd already had three sons—John Jr., who was then twelve; Robert, who was nine; and Franklin, who was six—and they'd waited a long time before they'd decided to try once more for a girl. They found out right away I was a boy. I wore my hair shorter then.*

My father and my high school football coach, Larry Bruno, who was the chairman of Joe Namath Day, shared the limousine I rode in. It was a nice limousine, and the boy who was driving, an end on the high school team in 1968, told me his father owned it. I was a little surprised. Beaver Falls isn't a very wealthy town, and not too many people own limousines. Then somebody told me the boy's father owns the local funeral parlor.

We drove northwest, a pretty, winding drive, past Ambridge and Aliquippa and Freedom and Monaca—great football country, the home of more All-Americans per square mile, I'll bet, than any other section of the country. Just a few miles before Beaver Falls, we cruised through

**120**

Rochester, the hometown of Babe Parilli, my fellow quarterback on the New York Jets. I didn't know Babe back home. I never did hang around much with older people.

*Every day, when I was in fourth grade at St. Mary's Grammar School, I used to pass an Army & Navy Store on my way to lunch. In the window of the store was a gold football helmet with the name Babe Parilli written across it. Babe was a pro football player then, and I was nine years old.*

In New Brighton, the last town before Beaver Falls, we drove by the drugstore where my mother works as a saleslady. She works now because she wants to; she used to work because she had to.

*When I was growing up, my mother was a maid up in Patterson Heights, the fancy section of Beaver Falls. At night, she'd stay up late, cutting down my brothers' old baseball and football uniforms to fit me. Now my mother lives up in Patterson Heights.*

We crossed a bridge over the Beaver River, separating New Brighton and Beaver Falls. From the limousine we could see the railroad trestle connecting the two towns.

*When I was a little kid, my best friend, a black kid named Linwood Alford, and I once walked across the*

**121**

*trestle. A train came by, and we had to hang on to the railing, just about four feet clear of the train. A neighbor, riding on a bus, saw us and told my father. He beat the hell out of me. He really believed in discipline. So did my mother. Till I was thirteen, I thought my name was "Shut up."*

The line of limousines turned into a place called Sahli Chevrolet, and most of us transferred into Chevy convertibles for a parade through the center of town. Weeb Ewbank—"Weeb who?" Don Maynard shouted—sat atop the back of one convertible. George Sauer trailed in another, Maynard in another, Johnny Sample in another. I followed them in a green convertible. Just to be safe, we put the two tension-easers in an enclosed car. I wasn't sure Beaver Falls was ready for them. Then, with a police escort, we pulled out of Sahli Chevrolet.

*I still remember the last time I left Sahli Chevrolet with a police escort. I was a senior in high school, and our football team had just won the Western Pennsylvania championship, but they weren't honoring me. Sahli Chevrolet was on Seventh Avenue then, the main street of Beaver Falls, and there was a big helium balloon flying on its roof. Four of us—Wibby Glover, Whitey Harris, Red Christley and me—decided we'd climb up on the roof late one night, paint "Take 'em Tigers" in orange and black, the school colors, on the balloon, then take the balloon over to the high school. Someone must've spotted us sneaking up the fire escape to the roof because, the next thing we knew, we were surrounded by cops, waving guns. "Don't shoot," I said. They didn't shoot, but they did put us in jail, and Coach Bruno had to come and get us out.*

From Sahli Chevrolet, we swung around to Sixth Street, in the Lower End, my old neighborhood. A lot of the houses in the neighborhood had been torn down, but outside of that, things hadn't changed too much. Most of the people along Sixth Street were black.

*The Lower End was a black neighborhood during my childhood, and most of my friends were black. We ran in gangs and we had rock fights—maybe that's how I developed my arm—and we had a lot of fun. I didn't know anything about prejudice until, when I was nine years old, Linwood Alford and I walked into a pizzeria, and the lady who owned the pizzeria kicked him out. "We don't want your kind in here," she said. I really didn't know what she meant at first, but I left, too. I figured whatever Linwood was, I was the same kind.*

We drove slowly past the house I grew up in, a narrow, two-story white frame house with a red brick base.

*The thing I remember best about that house was that the bathroom was in the basement, and during the winter the basement was always freezing. I hated to get up in the morning to go to school, hated to get up and go down to that cold bathroom.*

.    .    .

Right next door to my old house, we passed a 7-Up plant.

*When I was a kid, I once got caught borrowing pop from the 7-Up place. We used to do a lot of borrowing, from the neighbors, from candy stores, just little things. Some of the kids used to borrow junk from the junkman. They'd borrow the junk from the back of the yard, then go around front and sell it to the junkman. He bought it, too. He wasn't the world's sharpest junkman.*

From the car in front, Johnny Sample kept yelling back to me, "When are we gonna reach town? This the main street?" Johnny grew up in Philadelphia, and I guess he wasn't exactly awed by the size of Beaver Falls.

*Beaver Falls is a steel-mill town. Newspapermen are always writing that I'm from a coal-mining town, which is about par for newspapermen. There are no coal mines in Beaver Falls. There are about 17,000 people, and more of them work in the steel mills than anywhere else.*

The parade turned onto Seventh Avenue, and I could hardly believe the crowds, six and seven deep, lining both sides of the street. Somebody told me that there were at least 25,000 people watching the parade, which means that, even if everyone in Beaver Falls showed up, almost another 10,000 people had come in from the neighboring towns. Kids poured all over the street, running up to the car and shaking my hand and touching me and asking for

**124**

my autograph, and I was really stunned. I'd expected a nice little parade, maybe 2,000 or 3,000 people, but this was fantastic. Damn, I enjoyed it. I must have recognized hundreds of people in the crowd. Wibby Glover, my old buddy, came off the sidewalk and I dragged him up on the car with me. The cop escorting the car was an old neighbor from Sixth Street. People I hadn't seen in eight or nine years kept popping out of the crowd, and after we'd gone four or five blocks along Seventh Avenue, I saw my mother standing on a corner. She came over and gave me a big kiss.

*My mother and my father split up when I was twelve years old, and eventually each of them remarried. I stayed close to both of them. My mother—her name is Rose Szolnoki now—raised me, and she had her hands full. I think she did a helluva job. She taught me to be polite and to respect my elders. She's a great lady, and she loves to talk. She talks very slowly and very properly. We have a running gag among my friends that whenever my mother calls on the phone she uses up the first three minutes just saying hello. And she does some of the funniest things in the world. When she watches the Jets play on television, she prays to two saints, one when we've got the ball and one when the other team's got the ball. She's the only person I know who has an offensive saint and a defensive saint.*

Kids were handing me scraps of paper to autograph, caps to autograph, baseball gloves to autograph, footballs to autograph, even a black wallet to autograph. Somebody

**125**

kept tugging on my sleeve, saying "Oh, Mr. Namath, please let me have your autograph. You're my hero. You're the greatest man in the world. Please let me have your autograph." I turned around, finally, and there was the tension-easer, in her see-through blouse, shaking up the whole population of Beaver Falls. I told her to get back to her own car before she got arrested.

Farther along Seventh Avenue, we passed the Blue Room, the local pool hall. I knew the place pretty well. I probably should have gotten my high school diploma from the Blue Room.

*When I was a high school senior, a coach from the University of Michigan came to talk to me about college. Somebody told him he could find me at the Blue Room. When he got there, I was out front, lying on the hood of a car. He didn't even bother to talk to me. I guess he decided I wasn't the University of Michigan type.*

After we got past the center of town, the crowd thinned out, and their screams faded away. I was able to relax for a minute. I was still surprised by the size of the turnout; Sample must've drawn the people. We drove by the Geneva College stadium, where we used to play our high school games, and we drove by the Babcock & Wilcox steel mill, where my father works as a roller in the No. 2 hot mill.

*My father was born in Hungary and came to the United States in 1921, when he was thirteen. He's a strong man.*

**126**

*He played a lot of baseball during his younger years, and he always encouraged me to play sports. When I was a kid, he'd buy me a new baseball glove before he'd buy himself a new shirt. He figured he didn't need a new shirt to work all day in the steel mill. When he was like the business manager of our Little League baseball team, we had our one big fight. Some kid did something wrong, and Dad started yelling at him. "Don't yell at him," I said. "He's trying. You're not the coach." Dad said, "Don't you talk back to me." I said, "Well, leave him alone. You're not the coach." I put up my hand to protect myself, in case Dad hit me. He thought I was going to hit him. We didn't talk for a month or two after that. Dad was really hurt.*

At the end of the parade, the whole party drove out to the Holiday Inn to check in and freshen up before the banquet planned by the Beaver Falls Area High School Booster Club. I had to sit through a brief press conference, a typical session of brilliant questions and brilliant answers. Someone asked me if I thought my outside interests were hurting my football. I didn't know whether he meant Bachelors III or Johnnie Walker Red. I was tempted to tell him the tension-easers weren't for me; they were for my friends. Instead, I played it straight, as straight as I can. "Well," I said, "they didn't seem to hurt me too much last year."

I needed a drink after the press conference. I went upstairs and had one, or two, with Coach Bruno and a few of the Boosters, and my brother Frank came up to visit me. Frank had come down from Detroit for the banquet. He's in the insurance business there.

*When I was a senior in high school, Frank once heard a ridiculous rumor that I'd been in a bar. I mean, it really was ridiculous. I didn't go into bars when I was in high school. Hell, I knew better than that. You can meet a lot of undesirables in bars.*

*But this rumor did have a little truth to it. I actually had gone into a bar, but only for a minute and only to get another kid to come out. I'd been hanging around with this kid—his sister was my girl friend—and I wanted him to go someplace with me.*

*It was right before the football season began, and the word spread through town pretty fast that I'd been seen in a bar. When Frank heard it, he drove right to the house where I was living with my mother. He was a little bit upset.*

*Frank practically ran into the house. "Hey, Joey," he said. "C'mon out to the alley. Right now."*

*"What do you want?" I said.*

*"I want to talk to you," Frank said.*

*I took a good look at him and I saw that he didn't have his teeth in. He must've thought I was some kind of a dope. Sure, he wanted to talk to me in the alley without his teeth in.*

*I went out to the alley anyway—my mother was in the house—but I walked out holding my hands high, up near my mouth. You learn that when you grow up in a good neighborhood. When you expect trouble, you keep your hands in front of your mouth. It's better for your teeth.*

*"Were you in that bar?" Frank said.*

*"Yeah," I said, "but . . ."*

*Frank didn't let me explain. My own brother tried to steal a punch on me, tried to sneak one in quick before I was ready. I caught the punch on my hands and fell back against the garage. He moved in on me. I bounced off the garage, hit him in the stomach and started to run. Frank was just about as tall as me and weighed a lot more; he'd been a lineman in high school and in college. I didn't want to mess with him.*

*I ran to the front of the house, jumped into a ten-year-old Ford I had and locked the doors.*

*"You better open that damn door," Frank shouted. He ran for the car.*

*For a change, my engine started without any trouble, and I pulled away from the house and headed uptown. Frank got into his car and chased me. I guess he really wanted to talk to me badly.*

*When I got uptown, I parked; Frank parked across the street from me. I hopped out of my car, he hopped out of his car and started walking toward me, but I didn't wait for him. I crossed over to the other side. Then he crossed back, and I ran away from him. Hell, on foot, he didn't have a chance.*

*Finally, after I shook him, I got back in my car and drove home. Frank showed up a few minutes later, still wanting to talk to me. Just to even up the conversation, I grabbed a butcher knife.*

*I waved the knife at Frank. "Listen, you sonovabitch," I screamed. "You better stay the hell away from me. You*

**129**

*ain't no brother of mine. You don't even want to listen to me. You won't even hear what I got to say."*

*I wasn't going to use the knife. Well, I don't think I was going to use the knife.*

*Frank had no choice. He had to hear me out. I told him the story about just going to get the other kid out of the bar, and he checked into it and found out I was telling the truth. He stopped being mad at me. He didn't want to hurt me in the first place; he wanted to help me. He just wanted to make sure I wasn't getting into bad habits.*

All the time I was chatting with Frank and with friends of mine who dropped in, Coach Bruno and the Boosters were after me to start getting dressed. They were afraid I'd miss the banquet. I don't blame them. I'm pretty bad about being on time for anything. I miss planes. I miss appointments. I guess that's probably my only vice.

Finally, I slipped into a green suit—soft green, not Jet green, to match my eyes—and rode over to the Geneva College field house for the banquet. I was stunned again. There were more than 1,300 people jammed into the field house. They'd paid ten dollars each to come to the dinner, which is a lot of money, especially considering that Geneva College is a dry campus. I don't think I'd pay ten dollars to go to any dinner where you can't drink, no matter who was the guest of honor.

The decorations in the field house were fantastic. They had a big map of the United States, with a green light showing Beaver Falls and a sign saying, "Thanks for putting us on the map." Red and green lights kept flashing on and off behind the dais spelling out the word "Broadway." The aisles on either side of the floor were labeled Broadway and Seventh Avenue, for the main streets of New York and Beaver Falls. There were pictures of me all over the field house, with Coach Bruno, in my high school uniform, in my professional uniform. My mother was there, and my father, and my three brothers. My oldest brother, John, really looked sharp. He was wearing his army dress uniform. He was the first quarterback in the family—all I remember about his football playing was that he wore No. 42—but as soon as he got out of high school, he joined the army. He's been in since 1950, in Korea and in Vietnam. He didn't like the idea of going into the mills any more than I did.

*I really like my brothers. They're good people. Hell, I owe a lot to them. While I was still a little kid, they'd already made Namath a sort of magic name in Beaver Falls.*

*The day I started junior high school, I sat down in my first class, and the teacher said, "Joe Namath? Are you related to Frank Namath?"*

*"Yes, ma'am," I said.*

*"And Bob Namath?"*

*"Yes, ma'am."*

*"And John Namath?"*

*"Yes, ma'am, they're my brothers."*

*"Well, then," the teacher said, "you come right down here in the front row where I can keep an eye on you, and you'd better keep quiet."*

· · ·

**131**

After the meal was served, with dinner music by Henry Garcia and the Tijuana Trumpets, a big group in Beaver Falls, the program opened with a film of highlights from the Super Bowl game. I didn't particularly like the movie —I thought it was slanted in favor of the National Football League—but I did like the way it turned out. Then Butch Newton, the president of the Booster Club, gave a short welcoming speech, the only really short speech of the night.

*The Beaver Falls Area High School Boosters do a lot for the football team, and one of the best things they do is send forty or fifty of the most promising players to a preseason training camp. When I was a sophomore in high school, trying out for the varsity for the first time, I wasn't invited to training camp. I wasn't considered promising enough.*

*I guess I wasn't really surprised. I'd played quarterback in junior high, but I was only five feet tall and 115 pounds then, and I could barely see over the line of scrimmage to where I was throwing. The only reason I got to play at all was that the first-string quarterback, a kid named Jake Lotz, got hurt.*

Then George Sauer, Johnny Sample and Don Maynard got up and gave speeches. George just talked for a couple of minutes, Johnny just talked for a little longer and then Don talked for a couple of hours. I mean, you give Don a free meal, and he feels he's got to give you your money's worth.

**132**

Clive Rush, who was our offensive coach in 1968 and is now the head coach of the Boston Patriots, presented a plaque to my mother, and she thanked him and Beaver Falls in a few thousand well-chosen words. I'd been pretty embarrassed by what the players had to say, but once my mother started talking I thought I was going to slide right under the head table. (My posture, I'll admit, always is a little weak.) But, damn, I've got to say she was pretty good. She must've rehearsed that speech for days.

Then Weeb Ewbank presented a plaque to my father, and Dad said, "Thanks." He isn't usually that quiet, but it was starting to get late.

After Phil Iselin, the president of the Jets, and State Senator Ernest Kline, the master of ceremonies, made a few remarks, Joe Tronzo, the sports editor of the *Beaver Falls News-Tribune*, got up and talked. Joe's known me a long time, back to the days when I was playing baseball for the Elks in the Little League.

*Baseball was my best game for a long time, and my favorite. I pitched a little, but mostly I played the outfield —my hero then was Roberto Clemente of the Pirates— and even when I was struggling to learn to play football, I could hit a baseball. I played first-string varsity for three years in high school and my last year, when our team won the Western Pennsylvania championship I hit about .450. Half a dozen major-league teams were interested in me. I got bonus offers of $20,000 and $25,000, and I heard rumors that I could have gotten as much as $50,000 if I'd turned pro. The scouts talked to my father, but he didn't*

**133**

*want to be the one to decide whether I'd play baseball or go to college. About six years earlier, my brother Frank could have gotten a $20,000 bonus to play baseball, but my father didn't tell him about the offer. My father had made up his mind that Frank was going to college. Frank stayed only a couple of years at the University of Kentucky; when he found out he could have had a baseball bonus, he was pretty angry. Dad told me to make up my own mind. I talked it over with my mother and my brothers, and my mother said she wanted to see me go to college. I did what she said, and I'm damn glad. Hell, if I hadn't gone to college, I never would have got to meet Pete Rozelle.*

Weeb Ewbank and Phil Iselin excused themselves in the middle of the dinner and left to go catch a plane home. Weeb probably had some movies he wanted to study. They missed the speech by the mayor of Beaver Falls, Howard Marshall. Mayor Marshall presented me with the keys to the city. It was nice of him to do that but, by then, I would have preferred a glass of Scotch.

*I wish the mayor had given me a key several years earlier, a key to the high school gymnasium. I always loved to play basketball. I played guard, and I could really jump. I could stuff a ball into the basket. In my senior year, I was the only white guy in the Beaver Falls starting lineup. The rest of the team was black kids from the Lower End, kids I'd been playing with for years. We had no place to play on Sundays, so one Sunday a few of us climbed*

**134**

*through a window into the high school gym. We just wanted
to play ball. We didn't hurt anything. But we got caught,
and we were arrested and charged with breaking and en-
tering, and we were expelled from school for three days.
The basketball coach was pretty unhappy with us. I never
did get along with him. He was from the old school, the
conservative style of play, and we liked razzle-dazzle, fast-
break, passing behind the back, all that jazz. I fooled
around a lot. I remember once some guy was guarding me
awful tight, sticking his hand in my face all the time, so,
finally, I took the ball and wound up and followed through
just like I was going to throw the ball right in his face.
Except, I held on to the ball. The coach took me out for
that. In the middle of the season, we were getting beat in
one game, and the coach decided to take me out for some
reason. I was disgusted. I didn't even stop at the bench.
I just walked straight down the stairs to the locker room.
I heard footsteps behind me, and there came Benny Single-
ton, with a big grin on his face. Benny and I were the
co-captains and the leading scorers on the team. "If you're
quitting, Joe," Benny said, "I'm quitting, too." We just did
it on impulse. I mean, I wasn't even in the restaurant business then, or anything.*

After a man from Mayer China presented me with a
souvenir plate, rimmed in gold and inscribed, "Joe Namath
Testimonial Dinner," and mentioned that I used to break
windows at his company's plant—I broke a lot of windows
as a kid, with baseballs, with footballs and with golf balls
—the athletic director of Beaver Falls Area High School,

Bill Ross, got his turn to speak. He announced that the
school was retiring my old jersey—No. 19, Johnny U's
number, from the days when people used to call me "Joey
U"—and he reminded everyone that he had been the coach
of the football team during my sophomore year, when I
wasn't invited to the pre-season training camp. "I was a
great judge of talent," Mr. Ross said, "and the next year
I wasn't coaching."

*Early in my sophomore season, I tried to quit the foot-
ball team. I just felt I was never going to make it in football
and I wanted to concentrate on getting ready for the basketball season. "I don't think it's a good idea," Mr. Ross said.
"I want you to stay on the team."*
*"But I don't have any future in football," I told him.*
*"I think you should stick with it," Mr. Ross said.*
*Mr. Ross gave me the idea that he thought someday I
might develop into a pretty good football player. I don't
know whether he really believed that or not. He didn't
believe it enough to use me at quarterback in a single
game. The one chance I got to play all year, I played
defensive halfback.*

I gave a little speech, thanking Bill Ross for persuading
me to keep playing football and thanking him, too, for
giving me my old No. 19 jersey.

*I had gotten the same jersey once before. During my
senior season, Coach Bruno told us that if we won the
Western Pennsylvania championship, he would give us our*

**136**

*orange-and-black jerseys to keep. We won the champion-ship, but Coach Bruno had to go back on his word. He said that the school board wouldn't let him give away the jerseys, that the school couldn't afford it. So a couple of other guys and I broke into the locker room and borrowed our jerseys. Eventually, the word of our little adventure spread around, and we had to give back the jerseys.*

Then I told a story about my days at the University of Alabama, how I didn't have much money there and I applied for a job working as a chauffeur for a very attractive lady who lived by herself in a big house. "There were a lot of candidates for the job," I told the people in Beaver Falls, "but, for some reason, I was picked. I was the lucky one. I drove the lady around, did chores for her and one day, when I was putting away some groceries, she called to me from upstairs and said, 'Joseph, come up to my room.'

"I was very polite. I always did what I was told. I went up to her room. I walked in, and she said, 'Joseph, take off my dress.' I was very obedient."

The audience in Beaver Falls began to stir a little nervously.

"Then she said, 'Joseph, take off my slip.' "

I could see my mother turning colors. "Don't worry, Mom," I said, interrupting my own story.

"Then the lady said, 'Joseph, take off my bra.' I obeyed.

"Then she said, 'Joseph, take off my panties.' "

My mother looked like she was trying to disappear. I thought she was going to cover her ears.

**137**

"Finally, the lady looked at me and said, 'Now, Joseph, don't let me ever catch you wearing my clothes again.' "

Even my mother laughed.

I was laughing, too, yet the whole evening had given me a new feeling for Beaver Falls. I really felt at home, comfortable, like I was with the people I cared about and the people who cared about me. I hadn't planned to say much about Beaver Falls, but I couldn't help myself. "Eventually," I said, "I hope to come back here someday and settle down. I don't like the things there are to do here because there aren't any. But when I do finally get married, and I hope it's sometime in the near future, and I want to get married and have a family, I want to live here."

Damn, I hope Suzie didn't hear that line about the near future.

*I'm glad I grew up in Beaver Falls. It was a great place to grow up, with good people, real people, and a river and woods and athletic fields and swimming pools and rock fights and junkyards, everything a kid could want. I remember funny things, and sad times. I remember once, at the golf course where I caddied, a member turning to a young black kid and saying, "Caddie, give me my spoon." The kid never heard of a spoon—hell, even I didn't know it was the No. 3 wood—and he turned the golf bag upside down looking for a spoon. "There ain't no spoon in here," he said, finally, "but I'll go back to the dining room and get you one."*

*I remember hunting once with a BB gun, and I shot a little bird, and I went over and picked it up, and the bird*

**138**

*was still alive and it looked right at me and then closed
its eyes and died. I never hunted again.*

Coach Bruno finally got his chance to talk. He presented me with a plaque, and coming from him, I really
appreciated it. He's a helluva man, a helluva football
coach, always thinking. He spent most of the dinner copy-
ing down plays that Clive Rush gave him.

*Larry Bruno became football coach at Beaver Falls my
junior year. I was second-string quarterback most of the
season, up from playing fifth-string in my sophomore year,
but Coach Bruno started me in the final game, against New
Brighton. We won by about fifty points, and I guess that's
when Coach Bruno and I and my teammates began thinking we might have a real good team the following year.*

*We had a great team, a team they still talk about up in
that area. We were the first Beaver Falls team in thirty-five
years to win the Western Pennsylvania Interscholastic
Athletic League title. We won nine straight games. We
won our first two easily. Then we played New Castle. We
hadn't beaten New Castle in forty years. We hadn't scored
a point against them in thirty years. We beat them, 39-0.
Then we had our closest game, beating Ambridge, 25-13.
I had my worst game statistically, only three completions
in fifteen passes, but after the game a doctor told me that
I'd played with a shoulder separation. He said I couldn't
play any more football all year. I went to an orthopedic
man, and I played the next week. We won our last five
games without any trouble. We had two great ends, Tom*

**139**

*Krzmienski and Tony Golmont, who later had pro tryouts. Eleven men on our team won college scholarships, and all eleven finished four years in college. We were fantastic.*

At the end of the ceremonies, I awarded the first Joe Namath Scholarship to a Beaver Falls High School senior football player. I hope the scholarship doesn't mean that he has to follow in my scholastic tradition.

*I wasn't exactly a fantastic student. I had close to a C average in high school, and I never worked very hard on my studies. Lots of times, my mother used to say to me, "Joey, why don't you stop playing sports, or just play one sport, and put in more time on your schoolwork." If I'd given up any sport, I'm sure I would have given up football.*

After the banquet, most of my family and friends retreated to a party at the Blackhawk Golf Course. We needed something to drink after all those speeches. I guess we drank up all the booze in sight, and then a bunch of us went over to my father's house to play a bowling game he's got in his basement. My brothers and I lied and cheated and yelled at each other, just like always, just having fun. I admired the new rug in my father's house. I'd given it to him as a birthday present.

*One of the best things about the success I've had is that I'm able to do little things for my family. Sometimes my mother and my father and my brothers try to stop me. They say, "No, you've done this and you've done that, don't*

**140**

*do anything more," and they really feel badly. Well, hell, that's what it's all about. What's it all for if you can't help your own family?*

*And, shoot, what I've done for them is like nothing next to what they've done for me. They've all helped to get me where I am. My brothers John and Bob teaching me how to throw a football. My brother Frank saving his shoeshine money to buy me a basketball for Christmas. My mother cutting down old uniforms for me. My father encouraging me and cheering me. Hell, if they were in the position I'm in, they'd do the same things for me. I know that. I absolutely know that.*

I got to sleep for a couple of hours early in the morning, and then I woke up around eight thirty and went over to my mother's house for breakfast. My brothers Frank and John were around, with their children, and I just relaxed a little, just enjoying the family.

Then my father picked me up to drive me to the Pittsburgh airport, and we gathered together the whole crew that was flying back to New York, my teammates, my friends, the photographers and the writers, the two tension-easers.

The short one had changed her outfit. She wasn't wearing a see-through blouse now. Hell, no. She was wearing see-through pants. She had come down to Sunday breakfast in the Holiday Inn in Beaver Falls, Pennsylvania, wearing her best bare-midriff harem suit.

I don't know if Beaver Falls'll ever be the same.

**141**

# 7

# Some of
# My Best Friends
# Are Arabs

I hang out with a beautiful bunch of guys. I mean, they're great, they really are. Nice guys. Like Albert Anastasia and Abe Reles and Frank Costello and Longy Zwillman and Willie Moretti.

If you go by what you read in some magazines, that's my set. You know, we all just sit around my apartment and shoot dice every day.

I'm afraid my real friends aren't quite so glamorous. Most of them don't even know how to shoot dice. My friends know how to have a good time, and that's why they're my friends. I like guys who enjoy a good laugh, who keep things moving, who don't take me or life too seriously. There's one exception—Mike Bite, one of my two lawyers. Mike takes me very seriously. Mike takes life very seriously. Hell, Mike takes breakfast very seriously.

I pick on Mike a lot. When he missed the trip to Beaver Falls for Joe Namath Day, I told him he was being dropped from the traveling squad. Mike was hurt. I suppose I really shouldn't needle him so much. I only do it for one reason. He deserves it.

I guess all my friends and I deserve each other. We're all a little crazy. And we're all bachelors. I don't understand why there aren't any married guys in our crowd. I don't understand why their wives don't want married guys hanging around with us.

Of all the guys I see much these days, the one I've known the longest is Al "Hatchet" Hassan. Al got his nickname when he was a little kid because he looked like a hatchet. He looks a helluva lot better now. He looks like an axe now. Al's of Syrian descent, and Mike Bite, who's Lebanese, gets very upset when Al tells him that a Lebanese is a Syrian with money. Hatchet teaches speech at the University of Maryland, and I know he's a good teacher. When I used to have to say the plural of "you," I usually just mumbled "younse." Now, thanks to Hatchet, I pronounce "younse" very clearly.

I met Hatchet when I was a senior in high school, traveling around inspecting college campuses. More than fifty colleges were after me—for my good looks, I guess—and one of them was Maryland. When I flew to Washington to visit the school, Hatchet met me at the airport. He was the student manager of the Maryland football team, and he came from New Castle, Pa., right near Beaver Falls,

**146**

and we hit it off right away. He'd heard about me from his friends back home, and he really wanted me to go to Maryland. After I met him, I went to a lot of other college campuses, and from every campus I sent Hatchet a postcard. I don't know why those postcards made him nervous.

I made trips to Michigan State, Arizona State, Indiana, Iowa, Miami, Minnesota, Notre Dame and a bunch of others. I really liked Notre Dame until I found out it was an all-boys' school. Somebody told me there was a girls' school right across the lake but, hell, I didn't want to swim after my women.

Maryland was my first choice. One of the reasons I preferred Maryland was Hatchet. Another was that I thought Maryland was down South. It's funny—now I can name every state and its capital and almost every country and its capital, but I guess I didn't have a very good sense of direction then.

In order to get into Maryland, I had to get a mark of 750 in a scholastic achievement exam. The first time I took the test, in the spring of my high school senior year, I scored in the low 730s. I decided to take the test again in August. When Hatchet came home for the summer, we spent almost every night together, running around, having fun looking forward to good times together at Maryland. Then I took the entrance exam again. Hatchet heard the result before I did. He phoned me and said, "You didn't make it, kid"— I had scored in the 740s this time—and he was damn near crying. I didn't feel too good myself. I was really disappointed.

Hatchet told me that the Maryland coaches were phon-

**147**

ing a few other schools to see about getting me in. One of the Maryland people got in touch with Alabama, and the next thing I knew, an Alabama coach was at my house with a letter of intent for me to sign. I signed. Alabama and Maryland were just about the only schools that offered me completely legal scholarships—full tuition and fees, room and board and $15-a-month laundry money. One school offered me $400 a month and $4,000 for a new car each year. I was tempted, but I turned it down.

Looking back now, I know that not getting into Maryland was one of the best things that ever happened to me. There's no way I could've learned as much football at Maryland as I did at Alabama.

But when I first got to Alabama, I wasn't too happy. I felt out of place. I don't know why. Don't all college freshmen wear straw hats and checker-square jackets? I must've thought fifteen times about quitting and taking a bonus and playing baseball. Early in my first year, I was studying one night—well, I was sitting at the desk, anyway—and a guy walked into my room. I had a picture of my girl from Beaver Falls on my dresser; she was the football queen, and in the picture she was surrounded by her court. The guy pointed at the picture and said, "That your girl, Joe?" I didn't even look up. I just said, "Yeah." I didn't realize he was pointing at one of the court, a black girl. The word got around that Joe Namath went with a black girl, and pretty soon people were calling me Nigger-lover and just plain Nigger. One of my teammates even told his parents, "You ought to see this nigger we got playing quarterback. This nigger's somethin' else." His parents

**148**

were pretty damn surprised when I took off my helmet after one game and they saw I was white. I wasn't a crusader or anything. Those people down there were just raised one way and I was raised another. I didn't care if a guy was black, white or purple. It made no difference to me.

I was homesick, and I probably would have left Alabama if it hadn't been for Ray Abruzzese. Ray's from Pennsylvania, too, from South Philly, and he'd already been at Alabama for three years, and he showed me around, introduced me to people, took care of me. Ray's one of the loosest people in the world. Nothing gets Ray up-tight.

I remember once Howard Cosell came over to see me in our apartment. Howard and I were sitting in the living room talking, and Howard was doing most of the talking, in his broadcast voice, telling me how lucky I was to have him visiting. Ray was asleep in his bedroom, and I guess Howard's voice woke him up. Ray came into the living room in his shorts, started walking toward the TV set, saw Howard and did sort of a double-take. "Oh, you're *here*," Ray said to Cosell. "I was just coming in to turn you off."

Ray played defensive halfback for the Jets my first three seasons, and we used to drive to and from practice together. We left our apartment in the rain one day, and Ray drove from 76th Street up to 94th without turning on the windshield wipers. "You gonna turn on the wipers?" I said. "It's raining pretty good."

"Oh, yeah, sure," Ray said.

He pushed the button to *wash* the windows. We drove

**149**

for a block or two like that, the rain coming down and Ray washing the windows. "Ray," I said, "why don't you push that other button?"

"Which one?"

"The one where it says wipers."

"Oh," said Ray. "I didn't know about that."

Ray sometimes gets lost driving in our own neighborhood. We live at 76th and First Avenue, and one afternoon he got off the East River Drive at 73rd Street and drove right past First Avenue, past Second Avenue, past Third Avenue. For a while, I didn't say a word. I just watched. When we reached Lexington Avenue, I said, "Ray, where you going?"

And Ray just looked around and busted out laughing. Ray's loose.

Once, when we were in school, Ray drove home to Philadelphia with Jimmy Walsh, who's now one of my lawyers. Somewhere in Georgia or South Carolina, Ray was driving and Jimmy was sleeping. Ray shook Jimmy and woke him up. "When we reach the next town," Ray said, "you drive for a while and I'll rest."

"OK," Jimmy said. "How far to the next town?"

"Just another couple of minutes," Ray said. "Just a mile or so. I passed a sign for it."

Jimmy sat there, waiting to take over, and five minutes went by, and then ten minutes, and Ray still hadn't reached a town. "Hey, Ray," Jimmy said, "you sure we're supposed to hit a town now?"

Ray had driven the road from Alabama to Philadelphia maybe fifty times. "I don't understand it," he said. "We

**150**

should be there by now. I know I saw that sign. I know it said just one mile to that town."

"What town?" Jimmy said.

"I remember the town," Ray said. "I always go through it. It's called . . . er . . . Litter Barrel."

Jimmy's been a friend of mine, too, ever since my first year at Alabama When he was in law school and I was a senior, we shared a house in Tuscaloosa. I needed a mature, stable influence; the trouble was, so did Jimmy. Jimmy comes from New Brunswick, New Jersey, and, through Ray and me, his mother became a real Jets fan. Jimmy's mother once said to Ray, "I watch all your games on television, and I always wave to you, but you never wave back."

"Sure I do, Mrs. Walsh," Ray said, "but you're always in the kitchen when I wave."

Ray really says these things. I'm not making them up. No one could make up Ray Abruzzese.

One of my other close friends at college was a native Alabaman, a guy called Hoot Owl—Jack Hicks, who was the student manager of the Alabama football team. I seem to get along well with student managers; Mike Bite was student manager of the Alabama team, too, in the 1950s.

I'll never forget one night Hoot Owl and I went out for a few beers, and we were heading back to the campus in this ten-year-old Ford we had, a four-door sedan with no doors. Hoot Owl was driving, and we were both sipping beers, and suddenly a cop car pulled us over. Hell, I grabbed Hoot Owl's beer can, and I threw his and mine underneath the car. We were stopped on a damn hill, and

**151**

those beer cans rolled right back out again. I picked them up quick and threw them under the car again, and they rolled back out once more. "That's all right," one of the two cops in the car said. "You don't have to bother with it."

Then he looked at me and said, "Well, hello, Pain-suhl-vain-i-a kid."

Hoot Owl and I got out of our car, and the cop started to search us. "What the hell you doin'?" I said. "What the hell is this?"

"Y'awl are drunk," the cop said.

"Bullshit," I said. "We only had two beers."

"And reckless driving," the cop said.

That Ford of ours couldn't do more than thirty-five miles an hour with a tailwind.

"Man," I said, "I never had anything against police—except, you know, a couple of guys I didn't like—but now I know why you mothers are cops. You couldn't get a job anywhere else." /

The cop got a little upset. I thought he was going to shoot me.

The two cops took Hoot Owl and me into the local jail, and Hoot Owl was really shook up. I lay down in the cell, put my hat over my eyes and tried to get some rest. But Hoot Owl kept pacing back and forth. When he paces, nobody else rests. He's about six feet tall and about 260 pounds.

"Damn, Joe, we gotta get out of here," Hoot Owl said. "We gotta get out of here."

"Oh, Jack," I said. "Sit down. Get some rest."

"*You* don't have to worry, Joe," he said. "Coach Bryant

**152**

gonna come and get you out. He gonna leave me here."

"Don't sweat it, Jack," I said. "I ain't leaving without you."

About ten minutes later, a cop came over and got Hoot Owl and sent him home and left me in the goldang cell. Hoot Owl didn't even say goodbye. He just took off.

After we finished school, Hoot Owl became a high school football coach in Alabama, and when I visited Birmingham a couple of months after the Super Bowl, somebody told me Hoot Owl was asking for a raise because his team had the finest record in the history of his school. "How'd they do?" I said. I figured they were undefeated or something like that.

"Won five and lost five," I was told. "Best record in the history of the school."

One time, Hoot Owl came up North, and he and I stayed with Jimmy Walsh in New Brunswick. Just outside of New Brunswick, there are two little towns, one called Metuchen, the other called Fords. Hoot Owl drove us up to New York one day, and as we pulled out of New Brunswick, he passed a sign: FORDS—TURN RIGHT.

Hoot Owl gave me a funny look and kept on driving, and his face got very serious, like he was thinking hard. "Joe," he said, finally, "how come you gotta turn right there if you're in a Ford?"

I'm glad Hoot Owl was driving a Chevy or we never would've gotten to New York.

I'd already been at the University of Alabama for a year or two when I met Mike Bite. We met on a golf course in Birmingham. Mike and his brother, Richard, are partners

**153**

in the Birmingham law firm of Bite, Bite & Bite. Richard went to college at Auburn. For two weeks each year, the week before and the week after the Auburn-Alabama football game, Mike and Richard don't talk to each other.

It isn't easy for Mike not to talk. He's at his absolute best on the golf course. He gives free lessons to anyone who plays with him. The only problem is that if Mike teaches anyone to play the way he does, the guy is in a lot of trouble. But Mike talks a great game. Sometimes, he'll be in a sand trap, off the green, lying maybe four on a par-four hole, and he'll start talking aloud to himself, like a play-by-play announcer. "C'mon, Arnie, baby," he'll tell himself. "They're measuring you for the green jacket now, Arnie. You can do it, Arnie, you can do it." Then Mike'll take his wedge back nice and smooth, and bring it forward nice and smooth, and forget to take any sand and knock the ball clear over the green into another sand trap.

Everybody picks on Mike, but he leaves himself open for it. We were having dinner once in a Lebanese restaurant in Miami, and Mike offered his comments on every single dish. "Mike," I said, "how's this place compare with other Lebanese restaurants?"

Mike thought the question over very carefully, weighing all the pros and cons. "Pretty good," he decided. "Pretty good."

"Mike," I said, "how many other Lebanese restaurants you been to?"

Mike thought for a while. "One," he said.

He and I and Hatchet went to Washington once—I was attending a Touchdown Club dinner—and we knew we

**154**

had to catch a plane out of Washington about five o'clock in the morning. The three of us were sharing a room, and after the banquet, I got to the room about midnight. Mike was in bed, asleep, and Hatchet was watching TV. Hatchet and I decided to have a little fun. We woke up Mike and said, "C'mon, Mike, we got to catch that plane. Let's go."

Mike jumped out of bed—he moves a lot like a speeded-up cartoon—and ran into the wall. Then he turned and ran into a chair. Finally, he bounced into the bathroom and showered and shaved and put on a suit and a tie, and when he came out of the bathroom, I was in bed and Hatchet was sitting in front of the television set, laughing like hell. Mike looked at his watch and saw he'd been tricked. "The hell with you," Mike said. "I'm not changing again." He went back to bed with his suit and tie on.

Mike was the lawyer who negotiated my original contract with the New York Jets, and I've got to say he did a helluva job. They finally came up with a total package of $427,000, and I don't know whether that was for me to play football or for Mike to keep quiet.

Just about the time I signed my contract, I met Joe Hirsch, who now shares the apartment in New York with me and Ray Abruzzese. I met Joe at his place of business, the race track. No, he doesn't book bets; at least, he's never booked any of my bets. Joe writes for the *Morning Telegraph*, which is read by known gamblers. We met because Mr. Werblin, who was then president of the Jets, suggested that Joe, an old friend of his, look me up and show me around. This was in Miami around the time of the

**155**

Orange Bowl game my senior year at Alabama, and Joe showed me the Miami Springs Villas, where he was living, and a few of the Eastern Air Lines stewardesses who were training at the Villas. Joe and I double-dated a couple of times, liked each other's company and decided we'd look for an apartment to share in New York. It was a good deal for me, because Joe doesn't spend much time in New York; he's usually traveling, following the horses wherever the action is. I've got one bedroom, and Joe and Ray split the other. When Joe and I are both in town, Ray sleeps someplace else. I don't know where exactly, but Ray always manages to find a place to sleep.

It's a good thing Joe gets to New York occasionally, because when he's in town we get the refrigerator stocked. Joe's very big on cold cuts from the delicatessen. He's also very big on keeping the ash trays clean and the apartment neat. Joe's a tall, lanky guy in his early forties. He's the only one of my close friends who's passed that forty mark; most of the others are around thirty, give or take a year, except for Mike Bite, who's in his late thirties, going on sixty. I still get along fine with Joe Hirsch; I'm always polite to elderly people.

Joe, like Mike, is completely dedicated to the game of golf, and he's probably the most consistent golfer I know. I mean, he's really steady, never above 111, never below 109. Joe may not play very well, but he also doesn't play very fast. In his finest day, he was clocked lining up a putt in two minutes flat. If Joe wrote at the same pace he reads greens, he'd have to work for a monthly.

The rest of the guys I run around with are guys I've met

**156**

in New York—Tad Dowd, Bobby Van and Bob Skaff. Tad's not too big, but he has enough energy for ten people. He's always bouncing around, chewing a cigar, offering his opinions on everything that happens. He's been in the promoting end of the boxing business and the music business, and he's always promoting something, and half the time he doesn't even know her name. Tad's called the Truth Merchant; he seems to know something he shouldn't know about everybody.

Bobby Van's about as relaxed as I am. We've gone to play softball, pedaling down Lexington Avenue on a bicycle built for two. Bobby's pretty loose most of the time, but I can tell when he's getting serious—he takes off his hairpiece.

Bob Skaff is the final third of my Arab legion. Like Mike Bite, Bob's Lebanese, even though we call him the Egyptian Prince, which makes him a little nervous on the streets of New York. Bob's vice-president of Liberty-United Artists Records and, on the surface, he seems like the sanest of my friends. But I'm not so sure. When he heard I was going up to Monticello Raceway for some charity event, Skaff said, "What are you going to do—make a speech at halftime?"

Van and Skaff and I all played on the Bachelors III softball team during the summer of 1969, and they're pretty good ballplayers. They can hit almost as good as me. Tad doesn't go in for softball, but he likes the other games we play.

There's got to be a million other guys I see now and then, people I know from Bachelors III, people I know from football, people I know from my other businesses,

**157**

people I just know. I don't see too many guys from Beaver Falls except when I'm visiting back home; Whitey Harris and Wibby Glover and a few of my other old friends come into New York occasionally, but they don't always get in touch with me. "We don't like to bother you, Joe," they say. Hell, I wish they'd realize they can't bother me; they're my friends.

One of the things I liked best about Bachelors III was that I could always find my friends there, and they could find me. The only trouble with all the free publicity Pete Rozelle gave Bachelors III was that it really got crowded, and some nights even people I knew well weren't able to get in the place.

I talked to Ray Abruzzese about the problem one day. "Ray," I said, "some guys I know couldn't get into Bachelors III the other night. We ought to do something so our friends can always get in. Maybe we ought to get cards made up for them or something like that."

"Yeah," Ray said. "Yeah. That's a helluva good idea. We gotta get some of them V.P.I. cards."

How can I get in trouble with friends like that?

# .8

# Nobody Loves a Rich Rookie

▀▀▀▀▀▀▀

One day in the summer of 1965, at the New York Jets' training camp in Peekskill, New York, everybody on the club had to run a lap around the football field—everybody except me. We'd just played a rookie game against the Boston rookies, and my knee and I were excused from running. I stood on the side of the field and watched. I felt pretty bad about everybody else running except me. Of course, the other guys felt even worse about it. They all knew about my big bonus contract, and a lot of them, naturally, were just a little resentful. "What's the matter, rookie?" somebody yelled at me. "You too good to run? Your money weighing you down?"

I sort of hung my head.

Hell, if somebody had taken a popularity poll in Peekskill that day, I couldn't even have beat out Weeb.

Sure, some of the Jets rode me when I first joined the team. I don't blame them. If I'd been a veteran with the Jets in 1965, I probably would have resented me, too. A lot of those guys had been with the club when it was the New York Titans, when every payday was a cliff-hanger, when nobody knew if his next pay check would clear the bank or bounce. If they hadn't resented my bonus, they wouldn't have been human.

The Jets were human. Well, most of them were human. I'm not so sure about Wahoo McDaniel, a veteran linebacker from Texas. He jumped on my back once when we were running laps, and I wanted to kill him, but most of the time he just talked. If he'd spent as much time working on his linebacking as he spent shooting off his mouth at me, Wahoo would have had a helluva year. I gave it back to him a little. One day, as I was walking toward my Lincoln Continental in the parking lot, I saw Wahoo getting into his Cadillac. "Hey, Wahoo," I yelled, "why don't you get rid of that compact and get yourself a real car?" I thought that was a pretty funny line, but Wahoo didn't even smile; that hurt me more than all the cracks he made.

Not all the veterans were hostile—Curley Johnson kidded me just as cheerfully as he kidded everybody else—but most of them didn't exactly go out of their way to make me feel at home. They kind of gave me the cold shoulder.

Just before the season began, we held a team meeting,

only the players, no coaches present. A few of the guys stood up and talked about what we had to do to have a winning season, and then Mike Hudock, the offensive captain, said, "Anybody got anything on his mind? Any complaints?"

Man, I knew I had to say something. Everybody was waiting for me to say something. I got up. I wasn't very diplomatic; I guess I never am. "Some of you guys don't like me," I said, "but I don't care, 'cause I don't like you. I mean, I don't know you very well, so I can't really like you or dislike you, but from the way you act, I don't like you. All I'm asking is that you don't judge me for the money or the publicity, that you let me get out on the field and play football. If you dislike me for anything other than the money, tell me now. Let me know. If worse comes to worse, we'll do something about it—whatever way we have to."

The guys let up. They let me prove myself on the field.

Three years later, the day before we opened the 1968 season, Clive Rush, our offensive coach, walked up to me on the field in Kansas City. The rest of the team was running a lap to loosen up; I was still watching.

Clive was a little red in the face, like he always is when he's feeling emotional. "Congratulations," he said.

I tried to remember what I'd done the night before, but I couldn't think of anything spectacular. "For what?" I said.

"You won it," Clive said.

"Won what?"

"The election," he said. "You're captain of the offensive team."

**163**

I was shocked. I was actually stunned. I was also pretty damn happy. I felt great. I could tell that between 1965 and 1968 my teammates had really changed their attitude toward me.

"What's the matter, Joe?" Curley Johnson yelled, as he ran by. "You too good to run?"

This time I threw back my head and laughed.


Next to my family, my friends and a healthy percentage of the female population, the people whose company I like best are my teammates. We really came together in 1968—no cliques, no friction, no resentment, all of us working like hell to win the championship of the American Football League and all of us working like hell to have a good time. Most of us were under thirty, and we kind of represented the younger generation. We were into what's happening today in clothes, in music, all that sort of stuff. We went through training camp listening to The Fifth Dimension singing "Stone Soul Picnic," and we went through the season listening to Glen Campbell singing "Wichita Lineman"—when I think of the 1968 season, I still think of those two songs before I think of anything else, even before I think of the Super Bowl game—and some of us dressed mod and a whole bunch of us grew mustaches from the day we lost to Denver until the day, a month and a half later, we clinched the Eastern Division title.

It was Verlon Biggs who suggested that we give up shaving until the championship was clinched—I think it

**164**

was Verlon; I have a little trouble catching his words—and Jim Hudson backed him up, and I went along and so did Bake Turner and Cornell Gordon and a few other guys, and it wasn't anything big, but it showed we were a group, we were together. That was the whole story of 1968, that was what made us champions—the unity we had, the confidence we all had in each other. Damn, we liked each other.

And we had all types. Take Don Maynard, for instance. Don is closer than nine is to ten; he just doesn't believe in spending money. I remember once, my second or third year, we played a game in Oakland, and we weren't flying out of town till five or six hours after the game. Weeb got us together in the locker room and told us that there'd be some buses outside the ballpark after the game to drive us to downtown San Francisco. Weeb said we'd all meet at the Sir Francis Drake Hotel at ten o'clock to go out to the airport. Everybody kind of liked the idea—it was a good chance to relax after the game—everybody except Don. He raised his hand. "Coach?"

Weeb looked at him. "Yeah, Don?"

"Coach, what do you expect me to do, sit in that lobby for four hours?" Don said. "Ain't you gonna give us some money to get a room so we can stretch out a while?"

The rest of the guys cracked up. They were all figuring on going out and having fun. Curley Johnson, the clown of the club, grabbed Weeb's hat and started passing it around the locker room. "C'mon," Curley said, "everybody chip in for ole Don." The guys started throwing money in the hat, and poor Don was so embarrassed he didn't even

**165**

take the collection. I mean, he really had to be embarrassed to pass up that collection.

When I first joined the Jets, I was a little leery of Don. I'd heard rumors that he broke pass patterns pretty often, that he didn't run the paths he was supposed to run. Well, hell, that was ridiculous. In my first four years with the Jets, I can remember Don breaking only one pattern he didn't have the right to break. He was supposed to run a W—go out, cut back toward the line, go out and cut back again—but he broke the pattern on his second cut. You can't do that; it's too late then. I threw the ball where I thought Don was going to be, and the defender was standing right there and intercepted. Every other time Don's broken a pattern, he's had a damn good reason. And he always signals me. He throws his hand up in the air when he's breaking a pattern, and I've got to read him, I've got to catch his signal. Of course, sometimes, when Don throws up his hand, I'm not sure whether he's breaking a pattern or asking for room money.

Randy Beverly and Cornell Gordon are the two imps of the locker room, always playing jokes, hiding my shoes and my shirts and my socks, always messing around. I ride Cornell pretty good. I call him "Little Weeb," and I tell him he looks like Weeb and he acts like Weeb, and he cringes every time I say it. He used to call me Little Sonny because I was friendly with Mr. Werblin, but never in front of Mr. Werblin. Randy and Cornell are roommates, and they're always clowning with me and my roomie, Jim Hudson.

Hud's a lot like myself, a lot like Ray Abruzzese and

**166**

Billy Mathis. We're kind of strange for football players; we believe in giving more than a half-a-dollar tip for a six-dollar dinner. Hud and I have had some funny times together. Once, when we had a day off after a game on the West Coast, we went to Las Vegas, and I was sitting at the bar, talking with a girl, and Jim walked over to me and said, "Joe, give me a hundred. We'll go partners."

"No, Jim," I said. "I don't feel like gambling tonight."

"You don't have to," Hud said. "Just give me a hundred and we'll go partners."

"Right, Jim, right. Here."

Hud came back fifteen minutes later. "Joe," he said. "Joe."

I said, "Yeah, Jim?"

"Give me another hundred. We'll go partners again."

"I don't want to gamble tonight."

"C'mon now, dammit, we're going to win."

"Right, Jim, right. Here."

Six times, Hudson came over and six times he collected $100 from me. "You don't know what in hell you're doing," I said. "I got to get into this."

So I walked over to the dice table, and somebody brought two stools for me and Jim to sit on. We needed the stools; Hudson had a dislocated hip, and I had a fractured cheekbone, and we were both a little weak. We were even weaker later.

I started betting and, pretty soon, we were up about $5,000. It must've been beginner's luck. "Hey, Joe," Hud said. "Let's go get a cup of coffee before the dice turn cold."

"Hell, no," I said. "Let's stay here while they're hot."

**167**

"C'mon, partner," Hud said. "C'mon, Joe. Let's get some coffee."

We drank some coffee, then went back to the table. We lost a little. It got to my turn to roll, and all of a sudden a lady walked right in front of me. "Where you going?" I said.

"I'd like to play," she said.

I gave her a funny look, and Hud gave her a funny look, but somebody said, "Oh, c'mon, Joe, let her roll."

"All right," I said. "You go ahead, lady."

Hudson and I were betting pretty good, and the lady proceeded to roll—in order, a snake eyes, a three, a box car, a four and then a seven, and, quick as that, Hudson and I were wiped out completely. We were down $100. That's the only time I ever wanted to strangle a lady.

I see Hudson a lot on the road, but back in New York, the teammate I see the most is Bill Mathis. Bill's a bachelor. I mean, he's a confirmed bachelor. The summer of 1968, he fell in love and he was engaged to get married. His girl left New York to go visit her mother, and one day Bill called her mother's house and asked to talk to his girl. The mother started crying, "Oh, Bill, oh, Bill, oh . . ."

"What's the matter?" Bill said.

"She left home," the mother managed to say.

"What do you mean—she left home?"

"She went off. Went off and got married. Married this old boy from down here."

"She did what!" Bill screamed. He was in shock.

A day or two later, after some good heavy drinking, Bill got a phone call from his ex-girl. "Bill," she said,

"I'm over in New Jersey with my husband, and I'd like to pick up the clothes of mine that are in your apartment. If you want your ring back, you've got to let us come over and get the clothes."

"Oh, yeah, sure," said Bill, still not quite sober. "C'mon over and get the clothes."

Bill told me the story a few days later, and he said, "Gosh darn, here I am, making a little bit of money, and I love her and everything, and she pulls up with this guy that ain't been washed in three weeks, pulls up in a Volkswagen that's falling apart. And I've got to help them load the car. The man just took my wife away from me, and I've got to help him load that beat-up Volkswagen."

Bill phoned Mr. Werblin and told him what had happened, and Mr. Werblin said, "Yeah, Bill, yeah, I'm sorry. I'm really sorry." And when Mr. Werblin got off the phone, he told me later, he fell off his chair laughing. Of course, it wasn't too funny to Bill at the time, but within a couple of weeks, after a few drinks and a few dates, he started laughing about it, too. But Bill's sworn off getting married completely.

Bill announced after the Super Bowl he was giving up football to work full time as a stockbroker, but he changed his mind after training camp opened. I told him I needed him more than the stock market did. He's a helluva guy, a real gentleman. When I first joined the Jets, everybody was talking about "the Birdman"—"The Birdman's coming in soon"—and I kept wondering, Who in hell's the Birdman? Mathis showed up at training camp a week late— in those days, I couldn't imagine anyone coming to camp

**169**

a week late—and everybody was so damn happy to see him. I took one look at his legs, and I knew why he was called the Birdman. Mathis'll tell you he doesn't have skinny legs, but he's lying.

Bill's a beautiful guy. I remember once, during a game, he and I got our signals crossed, and I thought he'd be back blocking for me, and he thought I wanted him to slip out in the flat for a pass. I got creamed. I almost got killed from the side where I thought Bill was. He came back to the huddle and he felt so bad he kept apologizing over and over, "Gee, I'm sorry, Joe. Gee, I'm sorry." I think the whole thing hurt him more than it hurt me.

Our whole club's like that, everybody pulling for everybody else. Winston Hill is another one of my favorites. Winston is so strong, so tough. I think he's the best offensive tackle in football, or at least one of the two or three best. There's nobody Winston can't block.

Before I roomed with Hudson, I had no regular roommate for a while, and when we were going to Birmingham to play an exhibition, Winston told Webb, "I want to room with Joe in Birmingham."

"You want to what?" Webb said.

Winston's black—best black tennis player in Texas history—and, you know, in Birmingham, they're not too big on integration.

"Hell, put us together, Coach," I told Weeb. "That'd be a lot of fun."

Weeb looked a little shook. I don't know what happened, but when we got down to Birmingham and got the rooming list, Winston and I weren't together.

**170**

We don't have any real trouble about race on our club any more, but a few years ago we had an incident that could've been real bad. A few of us were in a bar drinking, and one of the white veterans said to one of the young black players, "You know, you're all right. You're a pretty good guy. I like you. You're a Negro, you know, but that Snell's a nigger."

I was standing next to the two guys, and I couldn't believe I'd heard right. "Holy shit," I said, "don't start that shit."

The black guy said, "What do you mean, he's a nigger and I'm a Negro? What's that supposed to mean?" And he started giving the white guy hell, which he deserved.

The story leaked out among the players, and Matt Snell was ready to explode. The next day, we had a team meeting, and the white guy apologized, and Mr. Werblin gave him hell, too. "We don't want any of that stuff here," Mr. Werblin said. "That's like cancer. It grows and it grows and it kills you."

The meeting helped, but it took a long time to get Matt calmed down. He was really up-tight, and I don't blame him. Now, hell, Matt's got the respect of every man on the team. He's some football player. He can run—if he didn't have a bad knee, nobody'd touch him (Matt says the same thing about me)—and I've never seen anybody who blocks so good. Matt destroys people.

There's one guy who's not with us any more I can't forget—Abner Haynes, who joined us after the 1967 season started. In one game, against Kansas City, I gave the ball to Abner, and he got hit right at the line and spun around

**171**

and he looked up and lateraled the ball to me. I had no choice; I had to catch the ball. And then I saw big Ernie Ladd, all 295 pounds of him, coming at me, and I ducked and Ernie went right by me. Then I started running, running for my life, and when there was just one man between me and going all the way, I got knocked out of bounds. Weeb pulled Abner right out of the game, and Clive Rush phoned down to the bench and talked to Abner and said. "Abner, we just don't have that play in our playbook. We just don't do that." I wasn't upset. Hell, I got up laughing. I guess it was kind of nervous laughter; I was glad I was still alive.

A couple of weeks later, against San Diego, I came up to the line of scrimmage and I called an automatic, an end sweep to Abner, and I heard a low voice behind me saying, "Uh-uh, Joe, no, Joe, uh-uh." I said to myself, "Oh, no," and I took the snap and turned around and Abner was gone, out of sight. He didn't know the play and he wasn't going to take the ball nohow. I had to keep the ball and I went down the sidelines and got a first down, and Weeb took Abner out of the game again. Abner wasn't with us in 1968, and I kind of missed him. I lost a few laughs.

One time or another, all of my teammates make me laugh—Emerson Boozer, Curley Johnson, Randy Rasmussen, John Schmitt, every single one of them. They're a helluva bunch, all different kinds of guys, all interested in the same thing. I mean football. Off the field, shoot, it's every man for himself.

On the field, the way the game is, one man has to take charge. I've known that ever since high school, when one

**172**

of my teammates talked in the huddle and I called time out and walked over to Coach Bruno and told him to take that guy the hell out of the game. Of course, guys talk to me in the huddle now—guys like Sauer and Maynard and Lammons let me know when they can beat their man— but I've got to be in charge. (Except when Winston Hill or Dave Herman wants to talk. I'm not going to tell them to shut up; I'm not crazy. Besides, they both only say one thing: "I can get him. Don't worry, I can get him.")

It's important to me, playing quarterback, to have the total respect of my teammates. I'll never forget when, after the Orange Bowl game my senior year at Alabama, my teammates elected me captain—that's the way they do it at Alabama; it's sort of a post-season honor. I actually cried, I was so happy. That was by far the biggest thrill of my football career, at least until the Super Bowl, and I'm still not sure the Super Bowl topped it. That was a beautiful moment at Alabama.

I know I've got the same respect now from my Jets teammates that I had from my Alabama teammates. I didn't always have it; I didn't always deserve it. At the end of the 1967 season, when we elected our most valuable player, I came in about sixth or seventh in the voting. A lot of people thought I should have resented that. I wasn't resentful. I didn't have a good year. Hell, I wasn't the most valuable player on the team. I wasn't even in the top two in my own mind. I forget whether I voted for Maynard or Sauer, but it was one of them. Maynard won, and he deserved it.

Then, in 1968, my teammates did vote me the most

valuable player on the Jets, even before we played in the Super Bowl, and I was pretty damn proud of that. I really had their respect. I remember, ten days before the Super Bowl, we were all watching the movies of the League championship game against Oakland, and we all saw me throw the pass that George Atkinson intercepted.

A year earlier, two years earlier, somebody might've yelled out a crack about that pass, calling it weak or bad or something like that. But not in 1968. Hell, no. In 1968, my teammates respected me too much for that.

"Great pass, Joe," yelled Curley Johnson.

# 9

# From Bruno
# to Bryant
# to Houdini

It was early in the 1967 season, and at halftime the Boston Patriots were beating us pretty badly. In the locker room, Weeb was a little nervous, a little emotional. He wanted to fire us up for the second half. At the end of a brief pep talk, Weeb shouted, in all seriousness, "All right, you *Colts*, now get out there and win this *baseball* game!"

We cracked up. Some of the guys almost fell on the floor, they were laughing so damn hard. But we went out in the second half and, after trailing, 24-7, fought ourselves back into a 24-24 tie.

That's the funny thing about Weeb. Sometimes he may not know which team he's coaching, and sometimes he may not know which game we're playing but, damn, the man gets results. It's hard to argue with the results.

Weeb is the only head coach ever to win titles in both the National Football League and the American Football

League, but he does some of the strangest things. Once, before a game, he began giving us some static, telling us to make sure that we had enough guys out on the field for special teams, the kickoff team and the punting team, things like that. "If we don't have eleven men out there, if we've got only nine or ten," Weeb said, "I want somebody to yell and scream and make sure we get eleven. But if we've got twelve men out there and nobody else says anything"—Weeb's voice got real low—"then don't you say nothing." I couldn't believe it.

Lots of times, I have trouble believing what Weeb tells me. I've always had the feeling that he'd lie to me in a minute, that I couldn't accept anything he said. Most of my teammates feel the same way; Weeb just drives Jim Hudson up a wall. But if you ever accuse Weeb of lying, he'll look at you and say, "Now, when have I ever lied to you?" You'll stop and think and you won't be able to remember one specific lie. Weeb always manages to slip out of it. That's why we call him Houdini. He's a goldang magician.

Weeb really gets me mad sometimes. I remember he complained to the press once that I didn't eat the ball often enough, and I was really pissed off. "Let him eat the ball," I said. I didn't mean that; Weeb's got enough weight on him already.

But, with all my arguments with him, I've got to give Weeb credit. He works like hell. He works harder than anyone I've ever seen. He's always the first man at the stadium and he's always the last man to leave. Day and night, he drives himself. I can't help feeling that football is like his whole life.

**178**

I've got to give Weeb credit, too, for knowing when to leave his players alone. He got a letter from the American Football League office in the middle of the 1968 season telling him to tell the Jets who were growing long sideburns and mustaches to shave them off. Weeb's from the crew-cut school of football, but he never even mentioned the letter to us till after we'd clinched the championship. He knew that if he'd told us to shave, we'd have suggested that he go do something else. Weeb could tell that we were serious about the thing, and that we were still football players, and we were winning, and we were all pulling together as a group. He had enough sense not to mess up that feeling we had going.

I guess what I'm saying about Weeb is that I love him one minute and I hate him the next, and that's the way just about every football player feels about his coach at one time or another. Hell, you don't exactly expect the coach to be your buddy. Couldn't you just see me and Weeb going out swinging together one night? Poor Weeb'd never be the same again. (Incidentally, at the New York football writers' banquet after the Super Bowl, Pat Henry, the comedian, was one of the speakers, and he said that, during the season, Weeb sleeps under my bed and pushes it up and down all night so that I won't strain my knees. That was pretty funny, but it was also pretty ridiculous. I mean, Weeb's got assistant coaches who can handle jobs like that.)

Of all the coaches I've had, I suppose the only one I never really hated was Larry Bruno, my coach at Beaver Falls High School. Mr. Bruno was the first football coach to show a lot of confidence in me, both as a player and as

**179**

a leader. I've played for dozens of coaches now—in college, in the pros, in All-Star games—and I put Larry Bruno up there with any of them. I know damn well that if I ever became a coach, I'd want to have Mr. Bruno working with me. He knows football. He works hard. He knows how to handle people.

I remember after the first game my senior year in high school, after we beat Midland, 43-13—and we'd expected Midland to give us a tough game—Mr. Bruno realized that we had a chance for a helluva season. The game was played on Friday night, and he decided to call a practice session for Saturday morning. He thought it'd be good to have us loosen up, and he also thought it'd give him a chance to check right away on injuries. "Joe," he told me in the locker room, "when we get on the team bus, I'm going to announce a practice for tomorrow morning. Now, I want you to let out a big cheer, 'cause I know that if you're enthusiastic about practicing, everyone else will be, too." I did what Mr. Bruno asked me to do. I let out a cheer, and soon everybody was cheering, and we held practices every Saturday all year. I actually enjoyed going to those practices. Of course, that was before I learned how to celebrate after a game.

Mr. Bruno worked on my quarterbacking. He spotted me taking a false step each time I got the snap from center. I took sort of a little step back with my left foot, then really moved back with my right. Mr. Bruno got me to cut out the false step, to stop wasting that fraction of a second. He broke me of a bad habit.

When I left Beaver Falls and went off to college, I met Paul Bryant, the Alabama coach, my first day in Tusca-

**180**

loosa. Somebody took me out to football practice, and Coach Bryant was up in the observation tower, watching and frowning and yelling. He waved his arms at me, so I climbed up the tower to him. He introduced himself, I introduced myself and we started talking. I didn't know what in hell he was talking about. We must've talked for fifteen minutes, and out of the whole conversation I only understood one word: He kept saying "Stud," talking about the ballplayers on the field.

Pretty soon after that, once I started practicing with the freshman team, I got to understand Coach Bryant. He made sure I understood him. The freshmen were scrimmaging the varsity third team one Monday night, and I ran to my left on an option play, and as I started to pitch out, somebody tackled me and the ball fell loose. I didn't make a scramble for the ball. Hell, I couldn't; the guy who'd tackled me was still holding me. Coach Bryant came out on the field and he said, "Goldarn it, Namath, it's not your job just to pitch the ball out and lay down there on the ground and not do anything. You don't just lay there." He kept grumbling, and I started walking back toward the huddle, just half-listening to him, not looking at him, and suddenly he grabbed hold of my face mask and nearly lifted me off the ground. "Namath," he said, "when I'm talking to you, boy, you say, 'Yes, sir,' and look me in the eye." I said, "Yes, sir, yes, sir." He scared me half to death. From then on, if Coach Bryant just said, "Joe," even if I was sixty yards down the field, I'd sprint up to him, stop a yard away, come to attention and say, "Yes, sir."

My sophomore year, when I was the starting quarter-

**181**

back, we were playing Vanderbilt, and I was having a miserable day. Coach Bryant pulled me out of the game, and I was really angry. I threw my helmet down as I came off the field. Then I went over to the bench and sat down, and Coach Bryant came over and sat down next to me and put his arm around me. To the crowd, it must've looked like he was cheering me up. Cheering me up, hell; he was damn near squeezing my head off. "Boy," he said, "don't let me ever see you come out of a ball game acting like that. Don't you ever do that again."

"Dammit, Coach," I said, "I'm not pissed off at you or at anybody else. I'm just pissed off at myself for playing so damn bad. I deserved to be taken out of the game."

"All right," Coach Bryant said. He understood me that time.

Coach Bryant is some man. I hated him at times, but outside my family and my close friends there's nobody in the world I respect more. He worked us so hard you just couldn't believe it. I know that if I'd been a tackle or a guard at Alabama, I wouldn't have lasted through college. Those guys used to come in after practice and walk straight into the shower with all their gear on, they were so beat. I felt guilty being able to stand up.

Victory is what Coach Bryant believes in ahead of everything else, and he measures everything on that basis. He's been asked whether I was the best quarterback he ever coached, and he says no, because Alabama lost four games in three years with me at quarterback; Pat Trammell ranks first with Coach Bryant, because Alabama lost only three games in the three years Pat played quarterback.

(But Coach Bryant does say that I'm the best *athlete*

**182**

he ever coached. I don't know about that, but I do know that I was the best *defensive* back he ever had. Well, one of the best, anyway. I'm not kidding. I was hell on defense.)

One thing I learned from Coach Bryant was that if you want to be first class, you've got to act first class. He always felt his team should have the best of everything, from the dorms we lived in to the hotels we stayed in. He wanted to make sure we believed we were the best, not cocky, but confident. I remember him saying lots of times before games, "Those ol' boys y'awl playin' jus' don't have the class y'awl got. Why, hell, y'awl are wearin' alligators while they're wearin' Thom McAn's."

Coach Bryant had a knack for throwing out funny lines at the most serious moments. Once, when some magazine came out with a story suggesting that the 1962 Alabama-Georgia game had been fixed—Coach Wally Butts of Georgia won a lot of money in a lawsuit over that story—Coach Bryant got hold of an early copy of the magazine and read the story out loud to us before practice. He got to the part where the magazine was trying to say that we'd been given the Georgia plays in advance and, because of that, we'd held them to only thirty-seven yards rushing in the whole game. Coach Bryant stopped right in the middle of reading that section. He shook his head. "Why, hell," he said, "that's just too damn many yards."

Babe Parilli played his college football for Coach Bryant, too—at the University of Kentucky in the olden days— and once in a while Coach Bryant used to get the two of us mixed up. I guess to him all Pennsylvanians looked alike. Before the start of the Orange Bowl game my sophomore season, Coach Bryant got the team together and

**183**

said, "Okay, we'll start off the same way we finished the Auburn game. Cotton, you go at halfback." He looked at me. "Babe, you go at quarterback." Coach Bryant stopped. "Now what the hell am I sayin'?" he said. Shoot, I could see him getting Babe and me mixed up on the field, but not with our helmets off.

Coach Bryant taught me a lot about football, but he didn't mess around much with my passing style. One time I was hurt and I was standing on the sidelines just throwing the ball around. I couldn't get a good spiral, a good bullet that would zip right in there. Each pass would wobble a bit. Coach Bryant moseyed up to me and watched for a while. "You know, Joe," he said, finally, "you're having a little trouble with your throwing."

"Yes, sir," I said. "I am."

He took the football out of my hands. "Well, it seems to me," he said, gripping the ball, "if you hold it this way and if you bring it up like this . . ." He stopped. "Oh, hell," he said, "what am I doing trying to tell you how to throw the damn ball? You've thrown ten times as many footballs as I have. What the hell can I tell you about throwing the football?" Coach Bryant flipped the ball back to me and walked away.

Coach Bryant and I had a very close relationship, a special relationship that's continued since I left college. I respect the man and I like him and I get together with him—to play golf, for a drink, to talk—every chance I get. I know how much it must've hurt him when, in my junior year, he suspended me from the Alabama football team. It must've hurt him almost as much as it hurt me.

The incident's been written about a lot, but nobody's

ever told the whole truth. What happened was that late in the season we had an open date, no game. Coach Bryant heard a rumor that I was drunk on Saturday afternoon and directing traffic in downtown Tuscaloosa. On Monday, we saw each other at lunch and he took me into one of the guest rooms in the athletic dormitory.

"Joe," he said, "somebody got in touch with me and said you were acting up Saturday afternoon. He said you'd been drinking and you were out directing traffic. I believe this gentleman for his word, but I'll take your word first 'cause I know you and I know you wouldn't lie to me. Is that story true?"

"No sir," I said. "That's a lie. I wasn't drunk and I wasn't directing traffic downtown Saturday afternoon. I was watching the Army-Navy game on television." I was telling him the truth. I *was* watching the Army-Navy game.

"Were you drinking at all Saturday?" Coach Bryant said.

He had a strict rule against any drinking during the football season, and I had broken the rule. I'd gone to a party Saturday night and I'd picked up a drink and I'd taken a few sips out of it. Not even a full glass.

"Well, yes, sir," I said. "I had a drink Saturday night."

When I said that, Coach Bryant really got upset. Not mean, just upset. "Oh, no," he said.

He thought for a while, and then he said. "Joe, I've got to suspend you." He told me to go to his office in the afternoon.

When I showed up at his office, Coach Bryant was waiting with his assistant coaches. "All the coaches except

**185**

one," he told me, "think we ought to punish you, but not suspend you. But I've made up my mind to suspend you, 'cause you've broken the rules, and I can't change that decision. If I did, or if the university changed my decision, I'd have to retire at the end of the season. I'd be breaking my own rules. I know we got two big games coming up and I know we need you, but if I let you play, I'd have to retire."

"Well, sir, I don't want you to do that," I said. I could understand the position he was in.

Coach Bryant suspended me. I had to move out of the athletic dormitory and I missed the last game of the regular season, against Miami, and I missed the Sugar Bowl game against Ole Miss. Both games were on national television, and it really hurt to miss them. Steve Sloan, who was a sophomore then, and Jack Hurlburt, a senior, took over the quarterbacking and did a helluva job and Alabama won both games.

After missing those games, I behaved myself all winter, and in the spring Coach Bryant let me come back out for football. I worked like hell and I won back the starting quarterback position. After my senior season, after I'd signed with the Jets, I walked up to Coach Bryant and said, "I want to tell you, you were right. You did the right thing, suspending me. And I want to thank you."

I had one final encounter with Coach Bryant before I left Tuscaloosa. He called me into his office one day and said, "Joe, I just heard about what a good baseball player you were. I never realized that. Why didn't you tell me, boy? Maybe I could have worked it out for you to play baseball here in the spring each year." Hell, yes, Coach

Bryant would have let me pass up spring football and play baseball instead—if I'd broken both legs and my throwing arm.

Coach Bryant seemed to know me, to understand me, better than any other coach I've played for. Now, Weeb Ewbank and I are on completely different wavelengths, except we both like to win. Weeb's wavelength is right for him, and mine is right for me; they just don't run together.

I still think Weeb was wrong back in 1967, during the exhibition season, when I got a lot of attention, most of it bad, for disappearing from training camp one night. I think Weeb should have given me permission to go away that night.

I had a lot of problems weighing on me, personal problems, family problems. I felt I had to get away by myself ·and think about them and work them out. I felt I had to get out of training camp, out of Peekskill, for at least a night. Of course, I felt I had to get out of Peekskill a lot of nights—if you've ever spent a night in Peekskill, you know what I mean—but this time I really felt kind of desperate to get away.

Before I left training camp, I went to Weeb and asked him for permission to go into New York City for the night. He turned me down, which didn't really surprise me. "I'm going anyway," I told him. "I'll just have to pay the fine, whatever it is. I'm going, but I'll be back tomorrow."

I went into New York, and I thought about my problems, and I thought about them over a few glasses of Scotch. I hit a few of my favorite spots, but no matter what you heard, I didn't hit the sports editor of *Time* magazine.

He filed a lawsuit accusing me of beating him up around three o'clock in the morning in a place called The Open End. I didn't. Hell, I've never won a decision from a sportswriter yet. The sports editor also said that I called him a "hundred-dollar-a-week creep," and he seemed almost as upset by the price as by anything else. I never called him that; I had no idea what his salary was.

The next day, I went back to training camp, and I got hit myself—with a fine of either $400 or $500, I forget which. (I do remember that I paid the fine eventually; the club didn't let me off the hook.) My teammates were pretty upset by my disappearance—I don't blame them—but the whole damn situation could have been avoided if Weeb had only understood me, if he'd realized how important it was for me to get away for a while, if he'd given me the night off. Instead, he got everybody all shook up. I met with all the veterans when I returned and explained that I hadn't run out on them, that they didn't have to worry about me disappearing in the middle of the season, that I just had some personal problems on my mind. I didn't go into any details; I didn't have to. My teammates accepted my explanation. They know me, and they know they can count on me, just like I can count on them.

Weeb and I had another pretty good disagreement the following summer, the week of our opening exhibition game against Houston. My left knee was hurting, and the Tuesday before the game I told Weeb I wasn't going to be able to play. I could have played if I'd gotten the knee all shot up with painkiller, but there didn't seem much sense in that just for an exhibition game. It wasn't worth the risk.

**188**

The game was being played in Houston, and there was a lot of pre-game interest and a fairly good ticket sale. The Texans had little pins made up showing a big guy stepping on a pair of white shoes—meaning me—and they were all excited. Well, Weeb should have told everyone on Tuesday or Wednesday that I wasn't going to play. But he was too worried about the damn ticket sales and the Jets' percentage of the sales.

When the game began, I was on the sidelines, wearing my street clothes, unable to play, and the crowd booed the hell out of me. Weeb had actually wanted me to suit up, to stand on the sidelines in my uniform. "I'm not going to play," I said. "Why the hell should I get dressed up?"

"You feel like part of the team," Weeb said.

He had to be kidding. I never heard anything so juvenile. He was just trying to save face, trying to put on something phony, like it was a last-minute decision for me not to play.

Stories went out that I'd made up my knee injury and that the real reason I wasn't playing was that I was holding out for more money for exhibitions, and those stories were just lies. I took a lot of abuse, and Weeb could have saved me from all of it just by announcing early in the week that I was hurt and couldn't play. That was one of the times I really hated Weeb.

I really think I could've thrown a punch at Weeb then, but most of the time I'd rather just put him on. Once, in practice, I threw a pass to the wrong place, right at a linebacker, and Weeb, naturally, got all upset. "No, Joe," he hollered. "Didn't you see that linebacker right where you threw?"

**189**

I wasn't going to give Weeb the satisfaction of being right. I didn't want to spoil him. "What linebacker, Weeb?" I said. I had my best innocent look on my face, and Weeb looked a little confused. "I mean, can't you see all right, Weeb? I said.

He got all flustered. "Gee, Joe," he said, "I'm sure there was a linebacker there."

He was ready to doubt his own eyes, and I was ready to fall down on the field laughing.

I put Weeb on lots of times, and sometimes I suspect he puts me on. At least I hope he's putting me on. He couldn't possibly be serious.

I remember early in 1969, after the professional football draft was announced, I noticed that the Pittsburgh Steelers had selected Terry Hanratty, the Notre Dame quarterback, in the second round. I was surprised nobody had grabbed Hanratty in the first round; I was surprised we'd passed him up. He could be a helluva football player. He's got a helluva head start, coming from western Pennsylvania.

The next time I saw Weeb, I asked him how come we didn't take Hanratty. "I'm not in very good shape," I said, "and Babe's getting older. We could use a young quarterback."

Weeb looked at me and said, "Oh, no, Joe. We couldn't take him."

"Why not?" I said.

"You know, Joe," said Weeb. "Hanratty's got a bad leg."

A bad leg! Imagine—telling me about a bad leg.

"Right, Weeb, right," I said. What else could I say to the man?

Houdini!

**190**

# 10

## I Owe It All
## to Two Sturdy Legs

I was a real triple-threat man in college. On the football field, I was a double-threat. I passed and I ran. I know it's hard to believe now, but I was a helluva runner. The first two games of my senior year at Alabama, I carried the ball twenty-two times, averaged five yards a carry, ran for five touchdowns and was leading the whole country in scoring. I could really scramble. I mean, hell, next to me, Fran Tarkenton could hardly move.

I ran all right in my third game, too, and then, in my fourth game, against North Carolina State, I started off concentrating on my passing. In the first quarter, I completed seven out of eight passes. On the first play of the second quarter, I called for the option play. I was going to

**193**

roll out to my right, run if I saw an opening and pass if I had to.

I rolled out, spotted an opening to the inside and started to cut back. As I cut, my right leg suddenly slipped out from under me. Nobody hit me. The leg just collapsed. I couldn't believe the pain. I knew I couldn't get up. I thought I'd been shot.

Ever since that day, I've been only a double-threat—and only a passer on the football field.


I have a pair of legs that only an orthopedic surgeon could love. I'm planning to give them to science, if my lawyers can figure out a tax deduction. The right knee is scarred and stiff; the left one supports a case of bursitis a helluva lot better than it supports me. I can't run, and when the weather's cold and damp, walking's a real adventure. My way of life is to avoid body contact—on the football field. Sometimes, when I'm caught in a situation where I have to run with the ball, Weeb chases me along the sidelines—I'm probably the only adult male he can beat in a fair race—and he shouts, "Get out of bounds! Get out of bounds!" He really sounds scared. I've got to say this for Weeb: I may get all the pain, but he does half the wincing.

My problems with my legs go back a long time, back to when I was about seven years old and I traveled with the baseball team my brother Frank was playing on. The team competed in some kind of state tournament in Doylestown, Pennsylvania, all the way across the state from Beaver Falls, and my father and I made the trip.

I got sick in Doylestown. My legs started to hurt something terrible, and I ran a high fever. My father was afraid I was coming down with polio. He took me to a doctor in Doylestown, and the doctor gave me a prescription, and the members of my brother's team took turns staying with me all night to give me my medicine.

The fever finally broke, and my legs felt better, until the following spring, when they started killing me again. I was put in the hospital for three weeks. I got a shot every day, and then I felt all right again. The next spring, the legs acted up again, and my father took me to an orthopedic man, who looked me over and said all I needed was exercise. Well, hell, in those days, I got more exercise than anybody in the world. I played every kind of game a kid could play, and I was always running. Anyway, the pains went away, and my legs didn't bother me for twelve years, not till that game during my senior year in college, when I tore some cartilage and ligaments in my right knee.

I made a couple of bad mistakes the day we played North Carolina State. For one thing, I forgot to wrap white tape around my football shoes, which I always did. For another, I wore a T-shirt under my uniform, which I never did. Ever since that day, I've been a little superstitious; I've always worn white shoes—they used to be taped until the Jets splurged and bought me white shoes—and no T-shirt. No sense taking any chances.

Right after I signed my contract with the Jets, they

**195**

sent me to the hospital for an operation on my right knee. Dr. James Nicholas, the team surgeon, went into my knee, cut out some torn cartilage, pleated a stretched ligament, removed a cyst that may have been in there since I had that trouble as a seven-year-old, then sewed me back up. The operation didn't hurt me at all; I was unconscious through the whole thing. But as soon as I woke up, Dr. Nicholas told me to lift my right leg. I thought he was putting me on. He wasn't. He told me I had to lift the leg right away to start getting it back in shape, and I did what he told me. I thought I'd die just from the pain. I had to keep lifting the damn leg fifty times a day, and then, after a few weeks, I had a forty-pound weight put on the leg and I had to lift that, too. I might have gotten depressed if there hadn't been a lot of pretty nurses around to cheer me up.

Dr. Nicholas gave me one piece of postoperative advice that was a little bit unusual. He told me that he didn't expect me to give up all my social activities, but that, at least for a while, whenever I was stretched out in a horizontal position, I should try to stay on my back. He said that'd be better for me than anything else. Shoot, I felt a little guilty sometimes, but I had to follow the doctor's orders. It didn't seem to bother anybody else too much.

I was really fortunate that there were a bunch of people around giving me incentive to get my leg back in shape and play football. Like Frank Ryan, the quarterback for the Cleveland Browns. "If he's worth four hundred thousand," said Ryan, who had heard about my contract with the Jets, "then I'm worth a million." I've been told that

Ryan has a doctorate in higher math, but, hell, anybody can make a mistake in simple arithmetic. Dave Hanner, who'd been playing tackle for the Green Bay Packers since I was in about kindergarten, had a comment, too. He said that he didn't see how anybody who got that much money would be willing to pay the price in professional football. I guess Hanner had taken a lot of physical punishment in all his years in pro football, and he just didn't know what he was talking about. I'd played four years for Paul Bryant; you don't play for him and not learn to pay the price. All that kind of talk just made me work a little harder to get ready for my rookie season.

During that first year, even though I tried not to, I suppose I must have favored my right leg, and because of that, I developed bursitis in the left knee. It was a vicious cycle. My second year, maybe I favored the left leg—the knee felt like the worst toothache I ever had—and in an exhibition game against the Houston Oilers, I got hit when I thought a play was dead, and the right knee got all banged up again. I still think the damn play was dead—and people wonder why I don't like exhibitions. I recovered in time to play the full season, but the right leg never did feel good. After the 1966 season, I had another operation on the right knee—some more torn cartilage was removed and a tendon shifted around—and then, in March 1968, I underwent an operation to repair a tendon in the left knee. Hell, that's enough medical history. I don't even like thinking about it.

There's no reason for me to keep talking about my injuries, about my problems. Everybody in pro football plays

**197**

with injuries, with aches, with pain. That's part of the game. Don Maynard went through the 1968 season hurting every bit as much as me, or even more. Matt Snell hurt, and Jim Hudson hurt, and most of the guys on the club hurt at one time or another, and nobody cried about it. Well, Weeb cried a little, but that doesn't count.

I'll admit I do worry sometimes about my health. But hell, everybody worries about his health sometimes. That's why I gave up smoking; that's why I get my five, six hours of sleep every night. Sure, I worry. I know how illness or injury can strike somebody without any warning. My brother Bob had a slipped spinal disc a few years ago, and he couldn't walk for a while; damn, I worried about him till he got better. And I had an uncle, a real big, healthy man who used to take me to Pittsburgh to watch the Pirates play, and one day, when he was in his thirties, he got up from a chair and just fell down. He collapsed. He was half-laughing as he lay on the floor. "This is silly," he kept saying. "I'm all right." His spine had given way, and three days later he died. I was about thirteen years old at the time, and I cried when I heard my uncle had died. Naturally, I worry about something happening to me. I wouldn't be human if I didn't. But I don't want any sympathy or pity or anything like that, at least not from any guys.

The one time I was really upset about all the attention my knee got was when I was found unfit for military service. People wrote me stupid, vicious letters, and some of them even sent letters to my mother, telling her that her son was a draft dodger. I could take the abuse, but it was

**198**

pretty damn unfair to my mother, whose oldest son, John, has fought in both the Korean and Vietnamese wars.

I was trapped in an impossible situation. If I'd said I wanted to go into the army, people would have said I was crazy, and if I'd said I didn't want to go into the army, people would have said I was a traitor. I couldn't say a goldang thing. All I could do was go take my physical and go along with whatever the army decided. The army examined me and decided that my knees disqualified me from the service, but because of all the publicity I got, I had to take the physical three different times. Every single one showed the same damn thing: My knees just weren't good enough for the army.

Whenever I'm tempted to feel a little sorry for myself now, I think about the trip I took to military hospitals in Japan and Okinawa and Hawaii after the Super Bowl victory. I learned right there that my problems were nothing. I saw guys with open wounds, guys who'd lost limbs, guys who'd really suffered. It made me realize how small my problems were, and it also made me wonder what the hell we're doing in that war in Vietnam. I don't know much about politics, and I don't take much of an interest in it, but I'd like to see that war end. I'd like to see all those guys come home in one piece.

I suppose as long as I play football people are going to be wondering about my knees and asking questions about them, but I'd just as soon forget the whole subject. There are other parts of the anatomy that are a helluva lot more interesting. I once spent a little time with a girl named Carole Doda, the girl who started the topless craze in San Francisco. She'd had one of those silicone operations, and, I'll tell you, her operation helped her game a lot more than my operations have helped mine. Now that's what I call an interesting operation; that's something worth talking about.

Goldang, next to that, a little knee surgery's nothing.

# 11

## You Don't Call Anyone Who Gives You $400,000 "Sonny"

The first time I met David A. Werblin, in December, 1964, I was scared, too scared to even talk money with him. The second time I met him, he offered me $300,000. I stopped being scared.

Mr. Werblin was then the president of the New York Jets—he had taken over the club a year earlier—and I was a senior at the University of Alabama. Our first meeting took place in a hotel room in Birmingham, and I didn't know much about Mr. Werblin at the time. I didn't know he'd been president of the Music Corporation of America; I didn't know about his long career in show business. All I knew was that he owned a professional football team, and that was enough for me. I wanted to play pro football, and I didn't care about how much money I got for it. Well, I mean, I didn't care a lot.

But I had the help of a couple of people who did care; Paul Bryant, my college coach, and Mike Bite, my lawyer. After our final game of the regular season, before I ever met Mr. Werblin, Coach Bryant walked up to me and said, "Joe, you know the scouts are going to come around now and start talking to you. Do you have any idea what you're going to ask for?"

"No," I said, "but I'd like to get around a hundred thousand dollars if I could." I'd heard that some players had gotten $100,000 the year before.

"Well," said Coach Bryant, "you go ahead and ask them for two hundred thousand."

"Two hundred thousand?" I said. Damn, I was afraid I might frighten everyone away.

"Well, hell, you may not get it," Coach Bryant said, "but it's a good place to start. You may only get a hundred and fifty thousand."

A few days later, two guys from the St. Louis Cardinals who had drafted me in the National Football League came to talk to me in my dormitory room. They wanted to know what I had in mind, what I'd like for signing, and I told them, "Two hundred thousand." They didn't say anything, but they seemed a little shook up. They didn't quite believe me. I asked them for a new car, too. Hell, everybody asks for a new car. Even if it's a million-dollar contract, you got to get that new car.

The people from the Cardinals thought it over for a while and then they got back to me and told me I could have $200,000 and the new car. They wanted me to sign right away. "I haven't talked to the Jets yet," I said. I went right to Coach Bryant and told him what had happened. "They went for it, huh?" he said. "Well, you got something pretty good going. You've got to talk to the Jets now."

Then I had my first meeting with Mr. Werblin, and he kind of looked me over and sized me up. The second meeting, he got down to business. "I don't want to get into a bidding war, Joe," he said, "but we really want you to play for us. We'll give you three hundred thousand to play for the Jets."

"Can I borrow a dime to call my lawyer?"

I didn't say that, but I did think it. The whole thing was getting too big for me. I knew I needed a lawyer, so I called Mike Bite. I'd known Mike for a couple of years, but I'd never used him as a lawyer. Hell, I'd never had any need for a lawyer. You don't call in a lawyer just for a speeding ticket or something like that.

"Mike, you handle it," I said. "It's too much for me."

I was so damn excited that night. I couldn't believe what was going on. I couldn't eat. I couldn't sleep. To me, $300,000 was more money than ever existed.

I wasn't committing myself to the Jets or to the Cardinals. Coach Bryant had told me not to accept anything from either of them till I made my choice, and I didn't. I didn't want to be indebted. I carried my independence to an extreme. Once, when Mr. Werblin offered to buy me a Coke, I insisted upon paying for it myself. It's a good thing he didn't offer to buy me Scotch; I don't think I could have

**205**

covered that. When Mr. Werblin asked me to go out to the West Coast to watch the Jets play San Diego and to talk with him some more, I agreed to go, but I paid my own plane fare. Mike Bite put up the money for me, and we both went out to California. We watched San Diego beat the Jets, 38-3. I thought the Jets stunk. I really did.

Mike took over the negotiations, and he got both the Jets and the Cardinals to keep raising their bids, first one, then the other. "Just like blowing in a balloon," Mike kept saying. "You got to go as far as you can without breaking it." I thought the balloon was going to pop any second and I was going to wind up with nothing, but Mike told me not to worry.

The negotiations with St. Louis got kind of confusing. After a while, Stormy Bidwell—he sure had a good name—the vice-president, who was dealing for the Cardinals, began checking each move with the president of the club, his brother, Charley Bidwell. Finally, Mike started talking directly to Charley Bidwell, and when the president of the team said that he couldn't give Mike an immediate answer, that he had to get back to him, we got the feeling the Cardinals might be fronting for someone else, someone like the New York Giants. We may have been wrong—I still don't know for sure—but it wasn't a secret that the Giants weren't too eager to see the Jets sign me.

In the American Football League draft, incidentally, I was originally supposed to be the choice of the Houston Oilers. But the Jets had traded for the right to negotiate with me, mostly, I guess, because they'd received a strong scouting report on me. The report was given to the press after I signed, and it showed I'd been rated in twelve different categories. I got a "2"—above average—in four categories and a "1"—outstanding—in eight. I was a little hurt by a "2" in character, but I was pretty happy with a "1" in intelligence. Damn, I hope my high school teachers saw that.

There were a few newspaper stories that the reason the Jets traded for me, and the reason St. Louis lost the bidding, was that I only wanted to play in New York City. Those stories were simply ridiculous. I didn't know enough about New York at the time to like it or dislike it, and I didn't know anything about St. Louis. If I'd known then what I know now, I would have taken the Jets' offer even if it had been smaller, but back in 1964, when the two clubs started bidding, I just made up my mind that I was going to accept the better offer.

And the Jets came up with the better offer. Mr. Werblin put together a package with a total value of $427,000. The key to the package was a guaranteed $307,000 for me, including a $7,000 Lincoln Continental, a $225,000 bonus and a salary of $25,000 a year for my first three seasons. I had a no-cut clause in my contract, and a no-trade clause, and all the bonus payments were deferred. I still haven't collected the first penny of my bonus.

Besides what he gave me, Mr. Werblin paid a $30,000 lawyer's fee to Mike Bite and hired two of my brothers, Bob and Frank, and my brother-in-law Tommy Sims, the husband of my adopted sister, Rita, as scouts for the Jets. They were to receive $10,000 a year each for three years, and they actually had to go out and scout.

Mr. Werblin and I came to an agreement during the time between Alabama's final regular-season game and the Orange Bowl game against Texas. I didn't sign any contract before the Orange Bowl game, before my college eligibility ran out, but I did give Mr. Werblin my word. As far as he was concerned and as far as I was concerned, that was just as good as any contract.

The day after the Orange Bowl game, Mr. Werblin called a big press conference in Miami and announced that I was signing with the New York Jets. He didn't give out the exact figures in my contract, but the press began writing about $400,000. Hell, for the press, that was pretty damn close. Of course, Mr. Werblin didn't try to discourage anyone from calling me a $400,000 quarterback. He was in the business of selling tickets, and the way ticket sales jumped up after all the publicity about my contract. I guess he knew what he was doing.

Some people, looking back after the Super Bowl, have said that Mr. Werblin got a helluva bargain when he signed me. Well, I won't argue with that. But I got a helluva bargain, too. A year earlier, Hoot Owl Hicks and I had been driving around the Alabama campus in a no-door Ford sedan, and when I left Mr. Werblin's press conference, I was driving a Jet-green Continental. I've got no complaints at all.

Right before the 1967 exhibition season began, a full year before my original contract expired, Mr. Werblin negotiated a new contract with me. At the time, I was a little worried about my knees, and Mr. Werblin, both as a friend and as a businessman, offered to relieve me of some of my worries. We signed a new agreement covering the 1968, 1969 and 1970 seasons, guaranteeing me almost as much as my whole original deal and again guaranteeing that I'd be paid even if I wasn't physically able to play. There were newspaper stories later that Mr. Werblin negotiated the new contract with me just before he sold his share of the Jets in the spring of 1968, but those stories weren't true. The contract was settled before the 1967 season opened.

I got to know Mr. Werblin pretty well after he signed me to my first Jet contract. I found out fast that just about everybody called him Sonny, but I've always called him Mr. Werblin, both to his face and behind his back. He took a lot of interest in me, as a business investment and as a person. When I moved to New York, he showed me around. He took me to places like "21"—that's because there was no Bachelors III then—and he often invited me to dinner at his apartment. He introduced me to prominent people in the show-business world, and he said beautiful things about me to the press. Sure, he was selling tickets every time he praised me, but he was also making me feel damn good.

Some of my Jet teammates didn't feel quite so good about my relationship with the boss, the president of the club. They felt I was his pet or something like that and I was getting special favors. I can understand their resentment, but, hell, I didn't ask to be his pet, and I didn't think I was getting any special treatment. I just appreciated what the man was doing for me. It's damn tough for a kid from Idaho or Nebraska or Alabama or Beaver Falls to adjust to a city like New York, and if I'd been a nineteenth-round draft choice, left all to myself, I don't know if I could have made the adjustment. At least, I don't know if I could have made the adjustment and still played decent football. Mr. Werblin helped make it easy for me. I genuinely liked him immediately, and I liked his wife, and I liked their sons, and they all tried to make me feel at home in New York.

When I started making my winter home in Miami, I spent a lot of time with Mr. Werblin there. Sometimes we went to the race track; you'd think with him owning horses and part of Monmouth Park, he could've given me one good tip. Sometimes we played golf; he's a very good golfer, compared to Joe Hirsch, anyway, and he doesn't talk much on the course, compared to Mike Bite. I had fun with Mr. Werblin. I got him into the habit of stocking plenty of Johnnie Walker Red in the bar in his home in Golden Beach.

My first three years with the Jets, I turned to Mr. Werblin fairly often for advice, about places to go, about things to do, and usually I listened to what he said. He gave me fiinancial advice, too, about endorsements, investments, almost everything. During my second year in New York, I thought about going into the restaurant business—into an East Side club, naturally—but Mr. Werblin talked me out of it. He didn't think I belonged in the restaurant business. I disagreed with him at first, but I listened to him. By 1968, when I invested in Bachelors III, Mr. Werblin had sold his

**210**

share of the Jets, but I still talked to him about my plans. He again advised me against going into the business, but I went ahead, anyway. "Hell," I told him, "I can't get in any trouble owning a restaurant."

Mr. Werblin also recommended that I not get involved in Broadway Joe's, the franchising operation, but I didn't listen to his advice then, either. I'm glad I didn't. I think Broadway Joe's is going to be a very successful company; it's my major business interest now.

Mr. Werblin and I are still friends—we'll probably be playing golf together in Florida as long as we both keep going there—but it isn't the kind of relationship some people have said it is. He isn't a father figure to me; I've got my own father. I'm not a puppet, and he isn't pulling the strings; he doesn't manipulate me. He isn't my main business adviser; I've got my lawyers, Mike Bite and Jimmy Walsh, for that.

When I decided to retire over the Bachelors III situation, I didn't talk to Mr. Werblin at all. I feel badly about that, and I know he feels badly about it. I should have called him—he's always been kind to me and kind to my parents —but I guess I knew that he'd try to talk me out of quitting, and I didn't want to hear that. We drifted apart during my retirement, and it was my fault. But I'm pretty sure we'll get back together.

I like Mr. Werblin, and I'm grateful to him. I respect him as a businessman, and I like to hear his thoughts about my business opportunities, especially in the show-business field. He's always been great about offering advice and information to help me and my attorneys, and he's

**211**

done it out of friendship, not looking for anything for himself.

But Mr. Werblin and I no longer have any business dealings. I feel kind of sorry for him. Now that he doesn't own a football team and he doesn't have me to worry about, he's got nothing to do except handle all the business affairs of a guy who works on television, a guy named Johnny Carson. Well, hell, I suppose Mr. Werblin'll find himself a star soon.

# 12

## I Am
## the Greatest
## ...Sometimes

When Mr. Werblin promised me the $427,000 package to join the Jets, he was really bidding blind. He had never seen me play a single game of football. But the night before the official signing he went to watch me in the Orange Bowl against Texas, and for more than a quarter I didn't even get into the game. Mr. Werblin must have been wondering what the hell he put up his money for. Finally, in the second quarter, Coach Bryant put me in, and before the game was over, I heard later, Mr. Werblin was jumping up and down and screaming, "I'm not paying him enough. I'm not paying him enough."

I don't understand why he didn't say that to me the following day.

In a way, the Orange Bowl game of January 1, 1965, was the best of my college career, and the worst. I almost didn't get to play at all. In practice, a few days before the game, I reinjured my right knee, the one I'd hurt against North Carolina State, and I thought I was only going to be a spectator.

Before the opening kickoff, I was standing on the sidelines between Coach Bryant and Jim Goostree, our team trainer, figuring on just watching a good ball game. Coach Bryant, looking straight at the field, not even glancing at Coach Goostree, said, "Jim, can he play?"

My head whipped around—I was so stunned—and Coach Bryant kept staring straight ahead. Coach Goostree looked at me, and I looked at Coach Bryant, and Coach Goostree said, "Yes, sir, I think so."

I didn't start the game, and Texas moved ahead of us, 14-0. I still don't know how the hell they did it. I mean, they didn't even have a quarterback; they just had Jim Hudson in there. For their second touchdown, Hud threw a sixty-nine-yard scoring pass to George Sauer. Damn, I would have made a helluva bet that night those two guys would never become my friends. The odds were even stronger against Pete Lammons; he intercepted two of my passes in the Orange Bowl.

I went into the game in the second quarter, and I threw a touchdown pass, but Texas scored again, and we were losing at the half, 21-7. I threw another touchdown pass in the third quarter, and in the fourth we added a field goal. With the score 21-17, with less than a minute to play, we had a first down on the Texas six-yard line.

Three times I sent our fullback into the line, and in three plays, he carried us to the one-yard line. On the final play of the game, I tried a quarterback sneak. I thought I

**216**

made it into the end zone, but the referee had his own opinion. Nobody put six points up on the scoreboard, so we lost, 21-17.

Personally, I didn't feel I had an especially good night, but, statistically, I'd had a helluva game. In the first Orange Bowl game to be televised nationally at night, before what had to be the largest audience of my college football career, I'd completed eighteen passes for 255 yards, both Alabama records, and I'd been named Most Valuable Player in the game. Still, I felt so damn bad afterward, and not only because my leg was aching, not only because I'd had a finger stuck in my eye and the eye was killing me. What hurt most was that we'd gone into the Orange Bowl undefeated, with ten straight victories in 1964, ranked first in the country. That's what made the defeat really painful.


I've had plenty of good games in my career, and I've had my share of miserable games. I don't think I ever played any worse—compared to what I should do—than in the game against Denver in 1968. We'd won three of our first four games—losing only to Buffalo, when I threw five interceptions, another great performance—and we came into the Denver game strong favorites. A victory over Denver would have put us in a commanding position to win the Eastern Division title. But, once again, I gave up five interceptions, and even though I completed twenty passes, a season high, I knew that I'd cost us the game. In the locker room afterward, I made only one comment to the newspapermen. "I stunk," I said, and I was being kind to myself.

**217**

. . .

I don't have a particularly good memory for games I've played. The game that generally sticks in my mind is the next game I'm going to play. That's the one that concerns me—what kind of defense I'll be facing, where the weaknesses are, which plays and which receivers will work best for me. My best games, from my point of view, aren't always the ones in which I did anything spectacular. Like I remember pretty well that, after the Denver game of 1968, I went four straight games without throwing a touchdown pass, completing barely forty-two percent of my passes, but those were beautiful games for me, because we won all four. (I allowed only three interceptions in those four games.) Yet there were some games over the years that were special—games that were turning points for me and for my teams.

In the third game of my senior season at Beaver Falls High, we played New Castle, a school three times as big as ours. As I've said earlier, we hadn't beaten New Castle in forty years and we hadn't even scored a point against them in thirty years. I went into the game with a twisted ankle, and Larry Bruno was afraid I might not be able to handle the punting the way I usually did. "Don't worry, Coach," I said. "We aren't going to punt."

We didn't, either. We scored our first touchdown against New Castle since the 1920s the first time we got the ball. We scored our second the second time we got the ball. I completed nine of thirteen passes for 183 yards, ran for 63 yards and scored two touchdowns. We beat New Castle,

**218**

39-0, and we were on our way to an undefeated season.

The first game of my college football career, we played the University of Georgia. I was a sophomore, moving in to replace an All-American quarterback, Pat Trammell, who had graduated. (Damn, I think of Pat and I feel sad. He died of cancer not long ago. He was a helluva leader. He went to medical school after he finished playing football, and he became a doctor, and then he found out he had cancer. Coach Bryant and I went to visit Pat in a hospital in New York, and he knew he was going to die, and he was still in good spirits. He was a helluva guy.)

I was a little nervous, of course, in my first college game. But I got over my nervousness pretty fast. Three minutes into the game, I threw my first touchdown pass, covering fifty-two yards. We had no trouble beating Georgia, 35-0—our defense was fantastic; we gave up only thirty-nine points all year—and I had a good day. I completed ten of fourteen passes for 179 yards and three touchdowns, and I ran for thirty-six yards, only one less than the whole Georgia team.

We were off to a strong start, and we kept rolling, winning our first eight games. Then Georgia Tech spoiled our chance for an undefeated season, and it was my fault. In the first eight games, I'd completed sixty percent of my passes and thrown only three interceptions; against Georgia Tech, I completed less than thirty percent of my passes and threw three interceptions. The first interception set up their only touchdown. We lost, 7-6, and the fact that we won our next two games, against Auburn and against Oklahoma in the Orange Bowl, didn't make me feel any better about my terrible performance.

**219**

. . .

I always had fun playing against Georgia. In the opening game my senior year, my first game since being suspended by Coach Bryant, I completed sixteen of twenty-one passes against Georgia, ran for fifty-five yards and three touchdowns, and after a 31-3 victory, was named college football's Back of the Week. The rest of the season was just about perfect, if you don't count the Orange Bowl game against Texas and a battered knee that would never heal.

When I was a rookie with the Jets, I had a lot to learn—like walking, for instance—and both the team and I got off to a miserable start. In the first few games, I felt like a rookie, and I passed like one. I kept missing receivers. Sometimes I threw over them and sometimes I threw under them, and I didn't really know when to throw the ball at a receiver and when to throw it away. If I'd had any thoughts that pro football was going to be a snap—and I hadn't—I would have lost them right away. We suffered through six straight games without a victory, and I had some great days, like completing five of twenty-one passes against the Oakland Raiders.

I didn't contribute much to our first victory, over Denver, but the following week, against Kansas City, I came into the game in the third quarter, with Kansas City leading, 10-6. I completed seven of sixteen passes, one of them for the touchdown that gave us a 13-10 victory. From that day on, right through the Super Bowl—except once when I was injured—I started every Jet game.

**220**

The next week, we won our third straight game, beating Boston, 30-20, and in the last quarter, with us protecting our lead, I directed a drive in which we controlled the ball for more than eight minutes. Coach Bryant and I talked on the telephone after the game, and he said, "Joe, you were a real pro in that one." I was beginning to feel like a pro. I was checking off plays better at the line of scrimmage. I wasn't throwing risky passes. I was starting, just starting, to get the feel of my receivers.

Then, in our fourth straight victory, 41-14 over Houston, I completed seventeen of twenty-six passes for 221 yards and four touchdowns, statistically the best performance of my rookie year. At the end of the season, I was voted the American Football League's Rookie of the Year, but I wasn't too impressed with either the award or my own showing for the year. I knew the voting didn't mean too much because my teammate, Verlon Biggs, who deserved the award just as much as me, didn't finish high up in the balloting, and I knew my own performance didn't mean too much because we ended up with a 5-8-1 record. I'd learned in high school and college that nothing really mattered if you didn't win. Hell, at Alabama my junior year, when we lost two games, the word was: Rebuild.

I'd like to tell you about what was actually the finest performance of my rookie season, but, shoot, I promised her I wouldn't.

At the start of my second season with the Jets, I was learning to walk again, thanks to a pre-season injury in an ex-

**221**

hibition against the Houston Oilers. We won our opening game, wthout much help from me, and then we played the Oilers in New York, before the largest crowd in the history of the American Football League. I wasn't too damn accurate with my passes—I completed only twelve of thirty-one—but I was pretty effective with the ones that did get to receivers. I threw five touchdown passes, two of them covering more than fifty yards, gained 283 yards and didn't allow a single interception. We killed Houston, 52-13.

We beat Denver the following week, and then we went to Boston and heard Weeb's halftime talk about the Colts and the baseball game. In the last quarter alone, as we came from seventeen points behind to gain a 24-24 tie, I completed fourteen of twenty-three passes for 206 yards and two touchdowns. I know you can't wait to hear another statistic: In one busy minute of play, I completed four passes. If I could do that all the time, I wouldn't bother mentioning it.

By defeating San Diego—only New York's second victory in thirteen games against the Chargers—we stretched our unbeaten streak to five, and looking back, I think we should have ended the season right there. We met Houston again the next week, and for the first time in my career, covering all my high school, college and pro games, my team didn't score a point. Houston didn't do anything different; I did. I threw four passes right into the hands of Houston defenders.

We lost, 24-0, and we lost our next three games in a row, and I deserve part of the credit for that, too. Against Buffalo, I had five passes intercepted. We stumbled on until

222

the final game of the year when, despite my spectacular hangover, I had my most efficient day of the season, completing fourteen of twenty-one passes for 287 yards and three touchdowns, helping us knock Boston out of the Eastern Division championship, 38-28.

I wound up the season leading the league in passes attempted, passes completed, yards gained passing and passes intercepted. I wasn't nearly as unhappy with my interceptions as I was with our team record. The season that had begun so well ended 6-6-2. The year before, as a rookie, I'd been named Most Valuable Player in the A.F.L. All-Star game; in 1966, I was hurt and didn't even get to play.


In 1967, my third professional season, I really knew what I was supposed to do on the football field. The only trouble was: I didn't always do it.

I had games you wouldn't believe, incredibly good and, more than once, incredibly bad. Our season actually split in half; the first seven games were pleasure, and the last seven were a pain. We won five and tied one of the first seven games, and I had only one miserable game during that stretch. In the one tie, against the Oilers, I equaled an American Football League record by throwing six interceptions. I did set a personal record that day by completing twenty-seven passes (in forty-nine attempts), but I was more valuable to Houston than to the Jets.

The rest of the first half of the season, I passed like a pro: twenty-two completions for 399 yards against Denver, twenty-three completions for 415 yards and three

**223**

touchdowns against Miami, thirteen completions in fifteen attempts in a rematch against Miami (I played only half the game), twenty-two completions for 362 yards against Boston, a record string of fifteen consecutive completions spanning the Miami and Boston games. Still, the most satisfying game was the one in which my statistics were the least impressive. Against the Oakland Raiders, I completed only nine of twenty-eight passes, none for touchdowns, and allowed two interceptions, a poor showing by any standards, but we won the game, 27-14, the only defeat Oakland suffered all year until the Super Bowl. Emerson Boozer and our pass defense were so good that day they made me forget my own problems.

In the eighth game of the year, against Kansas City, Boozer got hurt, and our season turned downhill. We lost four of our last seven games. I've said before, several times, that I don't really care about my personal performances—they don't mean a thing if we don't win—and there was one three-game stretch late in the season that proves my point perfectly. Against Denver, Kansas City and Oakland, on consecutive Sundays, I completed a total of sixty-five passes; I've never thrown that many completions in any other three consecutive games in my life. But we lost all three games. I had nine passes intercepted in those three games. Against Denver, when I set my own record of sixty attempted passes, I gave up four interceptions in a single quarter, and every interception led to a Denver touchdown. I was ridiculous.

I finished the season with a good day—eighteen completions and not a single interception in twenty-six attempts for 343 yards and four touchdowns against San

Diego—but by then it was too late. We had been eliminated from the Eastern Division race.

My performance against San Diego brought my season total up to 4007 yards gained passing; no passer in professional football history had ever gained 4000 yards before. Our team wound up with a record of 8-5-1, the first winning season in the history of the New York Jets—or Titans —and we had given some hint of what we were going to do in 1968.


I don't remember all the figures I'm quoting. I have to look them up. Hell, I don't even remember the point spread for most of the games.


I guess I came of age as a professional quarterback in 1968, probably because the New York Jets came of age as a team. I threw 111 fewer passes in 1968 than I threw in 1967. I had seventy-one fewer completions. I gained almost 900 fewer yards. I had eleven fewer touchdown passes. And, even with those ten interceptions against Buffalo and Denver, I allowed nine fewer interceptions.

I didn't have to pass so often or so desperately in 1968 because we had a balanced team. For the first time in the history of the Jets, we held the opposition to fewer than 300 points in a season. We had four talented receivers and four talented running backs. We had great blocking and great tackling. It all made playing quarterback a lot easier than it had ever been before.

If there was a decisive game, it had to be the opener against Kansas City. We were nursing a 20-19 lead with

**225**

six minutes to play. We had the ball on our own five-yard line. For six minutes, we kept control of the ball. We gained seventy yards while we ate up the clock. I passed only when I had to, and the rest of the time, Matt Snell and Boozer hit the line. When the game ended, we were on our way toward the championship, and for the rest of the season, I never had any one especially outstanding game, one in which I set any passing records. Every single one of the eleven victories, leading to the title game against Oakland, was a great game for me and for all my teammates.

At the end of the year, I collected a bunch of awards: Most Valuable Player in the American Football League, Most Valuable Player in the Super Bowl, Most Valuable Player on the Jets, the Hickok Belt as the outstanding professional athlete of the year and, finally, the George Halas Award as the most courageous player in pro football. I got that last award the same night Pete Rozelle told me that if I were smart I would take the safe way out and sell my interest in Bachelors III.

Better than all the statistics, better than all the awards and all the games I've played, I remember one piece of advice I received from a teammate during the 1968 season.

It was the week after we suffered our first loss of the year, to Buffalo, in the game in which I threw seven touchdown passes, four to our side and three to their side.

Now we were getting ready to play San Diego. "Hey, Joe," said Gerry Philbin. "Remember: We're wearing green this week."

# 13

---

# You Never
# Get Blitzed
# in the Press Box

> *The New York Jets would do well to trade Joe*
> *Namath right now . . . It is unlikely that the Jets*
> *can ever win with Namath and Ewbank out of*
> *harmony . . . One or the other should go . . ."*
> WILLIAM N. WALLACE, *Football Expert,*
> The New York Times, *August 15, 1968*

I think he may have been wrong.

Once, when some brilliant sportswriter asked me if I had majored in basket-weaving at the University of Alabama, I shook my head, "Naw, man," I said. "Journalism. It's easier."

I was only kidding when I said that. I had to be kidding because I didn't know too many sportswriters then. Now that I know a lot of them, I'm not kidding any more.

Take the so-called experts, and I mean radio and television guys as well as newspapermen. Most of them just don't know what the hell they're talking about. They don't know football at all. I throw 500 to 1000 passes a week during the football season, and I don't know everything there is to know about passing, so how could they know

**229**

everything about passing and running and blocking and tackling and receiving and strategy and all the things they pretend to know? Man, I hear those commentators—and read those writers—and whenever there's an interception, they say the quarterback was forcing the ball. Or he threw off the wrong foot. Or he was off-balance. They don't have the slightest idea what it's like to stand back there with seven guys coming after you and five guys blocking in front of you and everybody going all over the place. They just don't know. There are, really, two main reasons for interceptions: either you threw a bad pass or you misread the defense. I'd like to take every sportswriter and every commentator and put him through just one all-out blitz drill at the beginning of the season and then see what happens. I'd like to do that, except for one thing. I don't believe in capital punishment.

I remember once Dave Anderson of *The New York Times* wrote that on an interception I'd thrown a foolish pass. I like Dave—he's one newspaperman who actually works at his job—but he was being just plain ridiculous. I didn't throw a foolish pass. I threw the ball because I thought it was going to be a completed pass. It got intercepted because a Kansas City lineman hit my arm and caused a lousy pass, not a foolish one.

Well, I suppose Anderson is entitled to one foolish story.

The sportswriters that upset me the most are the ones who just don't work at their jobs. I realize that the sportswriters are necessary. I know it's a two-way street; they help me, and I help them. But, goldang, I want them to work as hard at their jobs as I work at mine. I'm conscientious. I'm a perfectionist. I want to do every little thing exactly right when I'm at work. And I think newspapermen ought to feel the same way. Some of them are so lazy I can't believe it. They just take somebody else's feature story or somebody else's column and lift things right out of it without checking a word with the subject. Damn, I haven't gotten my Alabama degree yet, so I guess I'm not quite qualified to teach journalism, but it seems to me that when you're writing about some guy, you ought to at least see your subject and talk to him. Hell, I know I'm not the easiest person in the world to find sometimes. Chase me. Leave messages. Find out when I'm available. I know it can be difficult—sure, there are times when I don't want to talk to any writers, just like there are times when they don't want to write about me—but, shit, completing a pass can be difficult, too. If a writer works at his job, and makes an honest effort to get to see me and get to know me and an honest effort to tell the truth, I'm going to help him. Without writers, athletes wouldn't get any publicity; without athletes, sportswriters wouldn't have a job. It might be a fair trade.

I admit I've got a hang-up about the press. I ought to realize that sometimes the sportswriters are just giving their opinions, and they're entitled to their opinions. But a lot of people read opinions as facts. That's the whole problem.

Hell, I used to believe everything I read in the papers, everything about politics and murders and Vietnam. I don't any more. How can I? When I know that newspaper-

**231**

men get me wrong, how can I trust them with more important things, like wars and elections? If writers would only make it clear when they're giving their opinions and when they're giving facts, I guess I wouldn't get so upset.

I'm still pissed off at Dick Young of the New York *Daily News*. Dick's a pretty funny writer, but if he wants to make jokes at my expense, he ought to at least get his facts right. He wrote a story saying that I made up my mind to retire from pro football in June 1969 while guzzling Scotch at the grand opening of Gerry Philbin's restaurant. Young wasn't at the grand opening. He wasn't at the press conference when I announced my retirement. And he never even tried to call me to ask me what had happened. If he had talked to me, I would have told him, first, that I'd made up my mind to retire before I got to Philbin's restaurant and, second, I only drank wine at the opening.

I'd guess that, of all the stories written about me, maybe ten percent, at best, have been really accurate. The rest screw up the facts or screw up quotes or screw up the interpretation. Lots of things are just out-and-out lies, complete inventions. One lady reporter once wrote that while she was interviewing me and asking me about my appeal I answered her by grabbing her hand and pressing it against me. She actually wrote that in a newspaper. There's no way I can answer something like that. I can just say one thing: Let go.

I'm being harsh on sportswriters—they don't all have wild imaginations like that lady—but I guess it's because they've been harsh on me. A guy named Jack Hairston in the *Jacksonville Journal* once called me "this creep" with "a million-dollar arm" and a "ten-cent head." And a guy named George Bugbee in the *Memphis Press-Scimitar*— a good name for his kind of paper—said, "He wears his hair in that mode so attractive to burrowing insects . . . I hope the wobble in his knee becomes an utter hobble."

And I get criticized for not always sitting down and talking with writers. Hell, I wouldn't want to sit down in the same room with anybody who would write stuff like that.

The guy I would like to sit down with is a writer from Boston named Al Hirshberg. I've never met the man, as far as I know, but he knows a helluva lot about me, or so he pretends. In 1968, *Esquire* magazine got Bill Mathis, my teammate and friend, to do a story about me. Bill did a conscientious job, asking me questions, trying to get some fresh material, and then *Esquire* took his story, and without telling him, had Al Hirshberg write his own little comments into the margin. His comments were mostly juvenile and mostly wrong:

"Is it possible that Joe Namath really believes that Weeb Ewbank ever compared him to Johnny Unitas?" (Maybe Weeb didn't. Maybe all those stories I've seen in the newspapers and magazines quoting Weeb comparing me and Johnny were just made up. I should know better than to believe what I read.)

"God almighty, here is this man extolling the joys of training camps, and he spends most of his life ducking out of them." (I left training camp without permission exactly once.)

"I doubt if Ewbank could ever tell Namath anything,

**233**

for Namath makes his own rules and ignores everybody else's." (Yeah. I made that rule about not associating with undesirable characters.)

"Namath owes the press far more than it owes him." (Would Hirshberg like to check the tabs at Bachelors III?)

"If it weren't for football, Namath wouldn't have been anything but a local yokel back home in Pennsylvania." (Shit, to get out of the steel mills, I'd have joined the Air Force or even, if I'd been real desperate, become a sportswriter.)

"Ah, humility, thy name is Namath." (Well, he's right about that.)

That's enough to give you a good idea of Hirshberg's kind of deep analysis. As Weeb says, that's what I've got to put up with. Anyway, the story hurt Bill Mathis more than it hurt me. He really got sandbagged. I was used to being abused.

I'm not saying all sportswriters or all sportscasters are like Hirshberg or Bugbee or Hairston. Hell, a lot of them are pretty decent guys, and a lot of them have been damn good to me. In fact, I'd say there have been more favorable stories about me than accurate stories. But let's face it: I've been pretty good to them, too. I mean, whether they like me or not, I give them something to write about. Like Bill Hartack and Muhammad Ali. Sportswriters are always putting those guys down, but if you took away all the stories that have been written about them, the papers would have a lot of empty space and a lot fewer readers.

It's funny. I've got a built-in resistance to sportswriters,

**234**

because of all the lies I've read about myself, but when I sit down with some of them individually, like a Dave Anderson or a Larry Merchant or a Jimmy Cannon, I enjoy myself. I mean, I could enjoy myself with Cannon if he'd get off the wagon and take a drink. A little less conversation and a little more Scotch, and we'd get along fine.

Just spending time with sportswriters is better than being interviewed by them. I'm interviewed out. I've been asked every kind of question, and I've given every kind of answer—straight, put-on, put-down, everything. Once in a while, an interview is fun—trading lines with Dick Cavett, say—but there just aren't any new questions to ask me. How's your arm? How's your knee? How's your head? How's your . . . Hell, I've been asked that, too.

What do you think of Earl Morrall?

What do you think of Weeb Ewbank?

What do you think of the Colts?

Of the Giants?

Of the Packers?

What do you really think of Weeb Ewbank?

The questions that bug me most are the ones that begin, "What if . . . ?" How the hell would I know, "What if . . .?" I suppose a few hundred people must have asked me by now, "What if you had lost the Super Bowl game? What would you have done?"

Hell, I don't know. I suppose I would have had a lot to drink, like I did when we won. I suppose I would have gotten a loser's check instead of a winner's check. I know I wouldn't have shot myself. What if I had shot myself? What would the writers have done? They'd have written stories, that's what. My question is about as good as theirs.

I remember one guy asking me once, "What if you had signed with the St. Louis Cardinals instead of the Jets? Do you think your life would be any different?"

I thought the question over very carefully. "Well," I said, "I wouldn't have as much chance to go to the Broadway theater."

He looked at me kind of funny. He wasn't sure whether I was being serious or not.

I remember another beautiful moment with a reporter, a lady from *Esquire* magazine. She called up a friend of mine—I happened to be sitting with him at the time—and said, "We're doing a story about Joe Namath, and could you give us the names of all the girls he's gone out with lately?"

Well, hell, the guy wasn't that good a friend, and besides he didn't have all day.

"Joe doesn't go out with girls," my friend said. "All that stuff about him and girls is just a cover-up. He's really a fag. He prefers boys."

"Oh, really?" said the reporter. She thought for a few seconds. "Could you give me *their* names then?" she said.

# 14

## I Should Have Studied Commerce

---

When I was in high school, earning a dollar an hour mowing baseball fields and scraping swimming pools, I once read a story about a man who found $80,000 that fell out of a Brink's truck. I remember thinking, "Why can't *I* find eighty thousand dollars?" I figured that was the only way I'd ever get that much money.

About ten years later, early in training camp for the 1969 football season, I was heading out to Hofstra College one night—trying to beat curfew or at least run it a dead heat—and Jimmy Walsh, my lawyer, was sitting in the back of a limousine with me. Jimmy was telling me about a chance to invest in a speculative new oil company in Texas. He talked about depletion allowances and tax

**239**

shelters and write-offs and he drew charts and quoted figures and kept saying I should put $100,000 into the company. He said that right away, because of the tax things involved, I'd be $80,000 ahead.

I kept looking around for the Brink's truck.

"Well, if you feel strongly about it, Jimmy," I said, "let's do it. Let's put $100,000 into it."

Then, with that out of the way, I leaned back and relaxed, trying to forget about high finance, looking forward to seeing my teammates again—the stock brokers, insurance salesmen, restaurant owners, real-estate dealers, bankers and night-club singers who make up the New York Jets.

Football players can't just be football players, not if they care about their futures. They have to be businessmen, too. Just about all of my teammates are involved in one or more businesses, and I am, too. I'm into dozens of different things, from oil to real estate, from slacks to stocks. This is one part of my life I never expected, I never really prepared for. I didn't study very hard in high school, and my only extracurricular activity, outside of sports, was the Audio-Visual Aids Club. I wanted to learn how to run a movie projector; I figured that was the only training I'd need for the football business.

In college, I wanted to study commerce, but I was advised to major in industrial arts. Industrial arts was a lot less difficult course, sort of glorified physical education, and I was told that the first thing I had to do was show

**240**

that I could handle my studies. By the time I got myself settled in industrial arts, I was just too lazy to switch into commerce. I had it easy, and I thought I'd probably end up in coaching, anyway, so I might as well take as many phys ed and teaching classes as I could. I made a helluva mistake.

But I've been lucky. I haven't gotten into any financial trouble—I don't count Las Vegas—because I've had good help and strong advice. Most of my business associates—starting with my lawyers, Jimmy Walsh and Mike Bite, and my main stock broker, my teammate Bill Mathis, and my insurance man, my brother Frank—are also my close friends, and I can trust them completely. I know they're always looking to do whatever's best for me. Hell, they don't know everything—they admit that—but when we get into a situation that requires special training, we bring in specialists to help us. We've used tax specialists and television specialists and advertising specialists and courtroom specialists, just about every kind of specialist imaginable. And everything is always set up to work for my future, to make certain that when I'm finished with football, my finances will be in good shape, that I'll never have to worry too much, not about money, anyway.

My biggest financial interest right now, as I've said, is Broadway Joe's. It's public knowledge that I own 145,000 shares of the company's stock; the stock opened at ten dollars and has fluctuated between eight and sixteen, so my share of that alone is worth more than a million dollars, maybe more than two million. I'm chairman of the board of Broadway Joe's, and I take an active part in board meetings, voting on every move we make, and I've tried to learn as much as possible about the business, down to how to prepare a Football Hero sandwich. I'm going to end up owning a few of the franchises, so I want to be damn sure I know everything I can about the actual operation of a fast-food restaurant. At least, I'll always know where my next meal's coming from.

I won't have to worry about sports shirts, either, for a long time, because I've got a contract for a Joe Namath knit shirt with Rex International, a division of Spartan Industries. Instead of a penguin or an alligator or any kind of animal on the chest, my shirts are going to have a little white football shoe set against a black felt background. We had to do a lot of thinking, of course, to come up with just the right symbol for a Joe Namath shirt. I mean, we considered using a little bottle of Scotch; we could have worked out a tie-in with Johnnie Walker Red, but the label wouldn't have looked good against a pink shirt. We thought about using a blonde in a bikini, but Suzie would have said that was bad for my image, and we thought about using a pair of dice, but Pete Rozelle would have said that was bad for football's image. I wonder, if anybody makes a bet wearing one of my shirts, is that guilt by association?

Another one of my businesses is an employment agency called Mantle Men and Namath Girls Inc. Mickey and I are partners, and I think I got the better half of the deal. I don't suppose we're going to be able to interview all of the applicants ourselves, but I think I'm liable to put more time into the business than Mickey. Eventually, we hope to open Mantle Men and Namath Girls agencies all around the country. That'll be kind of fun. I can imagine a tired businessman in San Francisco saying, "Send me a Namath Girl." And I can hear the employment agency telling him, "I'm sorry, sir, but we're all out of Namath Girls. Will you settle for a Mantle Man?" Between us, we should be able to fill any kind of office job in the world, as long as it doesn't require strong knees.

I have trouble keeping track of all the things Jimmy Walsh and Mike Bite have set up for me. There's the Joe Namath Snapper, a mechanical device that centers a football to a quarterback. The Snapper brings the ball right up in position for you to grab it and fade back and pass. It's a pretty handy little thing, and I enjoy fooling around with it. But I'm not ready to take it on the field with me, mostly because it doesn't know how to block. Maybe we'll come up with a John Schmitt toy to do the blocking. There's also a Joe Namath Football Game, an electronic game in which you actually set up your own offense and your own defense. I like the game; I've played it myself, and I'm not bad at calling defensive signals. The best part of the game is that you never get hit after the whistle. The second best part is that after you win a game you're allowed to drink in the locker room.

Occasionally, I make a television commercial, although I try not to do too many of them, because I don't want to get overexposed. I like to do commercials that are at least halfway believable. I mean, I don't think I'm going to endorse yogurt or floor wax or anything like that; it's not quite my image. And nobody's asked me yet to do a public-service message for the Boy Scouts of America. I did two

**243**

major commercials in 1968 that were kind of fun. One was the Schick commercial, when I shaved off my Fu Manchu, and the other was a Braniff Airlines commercial: "If you've got it, flaunt it." You'd be amazed how many people come up to me and quote that Braniff commercial. I don't mind hearing it at all, especially from a good-looking girl.

On a little larger scale, I've made a television special, sort of The World of Joe Namath, part documentary, part happening, and that's supposed to go on sometime during the 1969 season. I had to do some real hard acting for the special. I had to pretend I was a quarterback who liked girls and a good time. Actually, I've been on television quite a bit, I guess, for a guy who doesn't sing, dance or ride horses. Besides making a presentation on the Emmy Awards and besides always being interviewed on the sports news shows, I've done guest shots with Johnny Carson, Merv Griffin, Joey Bishop, Mike Douglas, Dick Cavett, just about every talk show except *Today*. Shoot, they do that *Today* show so damn early in the morning. They keep asking me to go on, and one of these days I'm going to stay up and do it.

I get a kick out of all the different things I do, all the things outside of football. I wouldn't do them if I didn't get some enjoyment out of them, as well as money. Sure, I like making money. I wouldn't mind putting away a few million dollars. But I don't do anything just for money. Well, hardly anything. Most of the time, there's got to be some fun mixed with the business, or I just won't bother with it.

Like take Bachelors III. I got into that mostly for fun;

I didn't realize quite how much fun it was going to be. Now I've got a feeling that Bachelors III is going to be a big thing nationally. I'm looking forward to having a spot in almost every big city where I can hang out, where I know I'll find my kind of people. I hope we get a bunch of football players connected with these places because I enjoy seeing football players. I even enjoy seeing defensive players.

My lawyers and I have a lot of different things in the works, but I want to look everything over carefully before I get involved. Besides the usual offers for endorsements and for investments that are guaranteed to make me a million dollars in three and a half days, we've been talking to people about a weekly television show and about a weekly radio show and about a syndicated newspaper column. I might do one or two of those things. I'd kind of like to be a newspaperman for a while and find out what it's like on the other side. Maybe I'll become an expert and start analyzing athletes. I'll explain what's wrong with Arnold Palmer's golf swing, and why Roberto Clemente isn't hitting, and how Jerry West needs work on his jump shot. Or maybe I'll become a broadcaster and ask gentle questions, the way Howard Cosell does. "Hello, my name is Joe Namath, and my guest today is Johnny Sample. Hello, John, welcome to the show. Is it true that you and Otto Graham are going into the used-car business together?"

I get a little dizzy just thinking about all the business possibilities. Basically, I'm still a football player, and that's the business I know best. But I almost got into a pretty exciting thing in 1969. I was part of a business group that was considering buying a gambling casino in Las Vegas. We finally decided not to buy it; it just didn't seem like a good enough investment. I'm a little sorry the deal fell through. Hell, if we had bought the casino, think of all the fun I could have had—meeting with Pete Rozelle.

# 15

## A Star Is Born

~~~~~~~~~~

Early in July 1969, during my temporary retirement from professional football, I changed my passing style. Nobody had fooled around with my passing technique since high school, but when I went out to Hollywood to make my first movie, a cameraman suggested that I release the ball a little higher. He wasn't worried about the trajectory or the velocity or anything like that. "If you let the ball go a little higher," he said, "we'll be able to see your face."

How come Weeb never thought of that?


Right after we won the Super Bowl, I was offered a number of movie opportunities. I could have signed a long-term contract with one of the studios. But my lawyers and I decided that it would be better just to sign for one movie and see how I do in that. If I liked it, and if the movie people liked me, then I'd do more films.

The picture we chose is called *Norwood,* and is based on a book written by the same guy who wrote *True Grit.* Hal Wallis, who produced *True Grit,* also produced *Norwood.* Glen Campbell and Kim Darby, who were in *True Grit,* are also in *Norwood.* John Wayne, who was the star of *True Grit,* isn't in *Norwood.* Instead of John Wayne, they got me. That's a little bit like trading George Sauer for an eight-round draft choice.

Glen Campbell plays Norwood, and I play his ex-marine buddy. My name in the picture is Joe William, and they didn't make up that name just for me. Joe William was the name of the character in the original book, which came out when I was still in college.

When I went out to Hollywood to do the film, I took a few of my friends with me—Jimmy Walsh, Bob Skaff, Al Hassan and Tad Dowd. We all stayed in a house in Beverly Hills that belonged to Skaff's brother. We also had rooms at a hotel in Beverly Hills just in case. Jimmy came along to make sure I had no problems with my contract; he left after a few days to go back to New York to negotiate with Pete Rozelle. Bob Skaff came along to check on the West Coast operations of his recording business. Al Hassan came along to serve as my personal acting coach. And Tad Dowd came along to act as a public relations man and as a scout. Tad kept his eyes open all the time, looking for opportunities.

**250**

My movie career almost ended very early. Flying from New York to Los Angeles, we ran into heavy turbulence, and I was ready to lay odds the plane was going down. I also got a little nervous because we headed south for a long time before we turned to the west. I thought I might be making my movie debut in Havana. The only thing that made me feel better was when the captain announced over the loudspeaker, "We are now flying over Louisville, the capital of Kentucky." I corrected him. I told him that Frankfort is the capital of Kentucky, and he apologized.

Our first night in Los Angeles, we decided to go to the big "in" discotheque, the Candy Store. We couldn't get in. We weren't members and we weren't with a member. I guess they were really impressed by my movie career. We turned around and went home to sleep at about midnight. That was probably the best thing that could have happened to us.

The next morning, I went to the studio, got lost on the lot, met Paul Nathan, the assistant producer, and got fitted for my wardrobe. That night, I stayed up with Al Hassan and rehearsed the lines for my first scene. We worked pretty hard. I wanted to act like a professional. I wanted to show up on the set knowing my lines. Hatchet coached me and taught me to pause between lines. The next day, I was on the set about eight o'clock in the morning, and at eight thirty, we started shooting. I read my lines nice and slowly, and Jack Haley Jr., the director, said "Joe, quickly with those lines, no pauses, please." I stopped and turned to Al Hassan and said, "Hatchet, you're fired." Al

**251**

was really upset. "Right up till then," he said, "I thought I was Mike Nichols."

I had maybe ten lines of dialogue, and we finished shooting the scene in half an hour, forty-five minutes. The movie people all seemed amazed that I actually knew my lines, that I didn't forget them on camera. I guess they expected an imbecile, a real buffoon—or, as Mike Bite says, a "baffoon."

I really enjoyed the people I was working with—Jack Haley Jr., Glen Campbell and the three girls who have the biggest female roles in the picture, Kim Darby and Meredith MacRae and Carol Lynley. Glen's a damn nice guy—he told me about all the troubles he had making *True Grit,* his first movie—and the girls were certainly better-looking teammates than I've had in a long time. George Sauer and Don Maynard may have great hands, but the girls had them beat in all the other physical equipment.

Don't get the idea that I had a huge role in *Norwood.* I didn't have to work like Lee J. Cobb playing King Lear. In the whole movie, I had about thirty or forty lines, spread out over half a dozen different scenes. It was a good way to start in the movie business, sort of like playing the last quarter of your first pro game. I mean, I wasn't just an extra. I wasn't just making an appearance. And I was playing a role, not just being myself. The scene with me throwing a football is a little one that takes place during a picnic. Everybody is kind of fooling around, and I throw a few passes through a rubber tire hanging on a tree. The Hollywood people expected me to be able to do that

252

every time. It isn't easy; you can't lob the ball because of the trajectory. Hell, I missed once or twice before I got loosened up.

Glen Campbell and I seemed to work pretty well together. We made up a few little things as we went along. We had one scene where we were meeting after not seeing each other for a long time, and we made up sort of a fancy handshake—back of the hands first, then upside-down—that Jack Haley Jr. really liked. Everybody on the set seemed to get along with everybody else, and Jack was very patient, not yelling at us, just helping us along.

On the Fourth of July weekend, I took off for Las Vegas for a couple of days to make my contribution to the State of Nevada. I had a good time in Vegas. I was able to forget about my problems with Bachelors III and Pete Rozelle, and I just relaxed. One night, Ted and Hatchet and Mike Bite, who'd flown in from Birmingham, and I went to see Little Richard, the singer, and he was wild, absolutely fantastic. He sang some of his great hits, and he wore a flowing pink robe, gold high-heeled pumps, and he just pranced all around the stage. During his act, he stopped and said, "We have a man out in the audience I'd like to introduce—Mr. Joe *Nimth*." Little Richard didn't even come close; he didn't know whether it was Nimth or Nemeth or Namath or what, but he was giggling away. "He's with the Jets," said Little Richard, in a real high voice, "and I'd sure like to Jet you, Joe." The whole place cracked up.

Then we went to see Dean Martin, and we got a table right at ringside. Everybody knows Dean Martin's re-

**253**

laxed, he's cool, but he's not so damn relaxed he's supposed to make you fall asleep. Mike Bite passed right out at the table, right in the middle of "Little Green Apples." There's Dean Martin putting on a great show, and there's my counselor, unconscious. I broke up laughing, but I had to cut Mike from the traveling squad again. I can't take him anywhere.

We flew back to Los Angeles Saturday night for a big party that Jack Haley Jr. was throwing. You couldn't believe that party, man. There were more good-looking broads in one place than I've ever seen in my life. Naturally, they all fell right in love with Hatchet, but he was already in love with Kim Darby; of course, he never told Kim he was in love with her, and I told him to forget her, that he couldn't take her back to his drama classes at the University of Maryland. Ursula Andress was at the party. She could be a helluva blocking back. In the first place, she's got some shoulders, and in the second place, no lineman would ever try to go around her. I didn't know the names of most of the girls; all I knew was they looked so good I even enjoyed conversations with them. I recognized some of the guys—Jean Paul Belmondo, Bill Dana, Tom Smothers—but I wasn't as interested in what they had to say.

Jack Haley Jr. has a fantastic house, built right on the edge of a cliff with his balcony extending out over the cliff. He's got a big swimming pool, heated to 100 degrees, and he's got stereo speakers in every room in the house. I thought of something while I was there. Jack's got a beautiful house and all the money he'll ever need, but he doesn't have the notoriety, the exposure, that I've got. He's striving for what I've got, and I'm striving for what he's got. I'm trying to get that house on the hill and all the comfort, and it's funny, but when I get it—if I get it— then I'll probably want something different, just like he does. Right now, he has all I want, and I've got all he wants, and there's no way we can trade.

During my second week in the movies, we went on location in the desert south of Los Angeles. When I wasn't busy on the set, I jogged a little, just enough to loosen me up, and I did sit-ups and I threw a football around with Hatchet and with some of the people in the cast. I thought about inviting a few of the girls to training camp if I went back to football, but I was afraid Weeb wouldn't go for that.

Right up to the end, I had no trouble at all learning my lines. I can memorize things pretty easily. The most difficult part of acting for me was to show emotions I didn't really feel—especially like laughing or smiling. I had to work hard at that. One time, when I had to look sort of disgusted, it was a snap. Glen Campbell and I were hitchhiking, and a beat-up old car stopped for me, and I had to look at it as though I was afraid to get into it. Hell, I *was* afraid to get into it. I had no problem looking that way.

When I saw the rushes, I wasn't too happy with the way I sounded. I've got a little speech impediment—I slur some of my words—and I'm going to have to work on that if I do any more films. I've also got to learn to keep my head up, not to look down when I'm talking. But I've got to admit I had no complaints about the way I looked on the screen. Damn, I looked good. I guess I'm photogenic. Well, I guess the camera doesn't lie.

I don't know what the critics are going to say about my acting debut. I think I did all right for my first time out, but I don't know what anyone else is going to say. The last I heard, Paul Newman wasn't worried yet.

# 16

# I Can't Wait
# Until Tomorrow

Late in the first half of an exhibition game against the St. Louis Cardinals, our second pre-season game of 1969, I faded back to pass to George Sauer. I raised my arm to throw, and as I came forward, my left knee suddenly buckled. No one had hit me, but my leg gave out, I slipped to the ground and the pass landed short of Sauer. My knee hurt like hell.

I spent the whole second half on the sidelines with my knee wrapped in ice. Nobody paid much attention, because Weeb had said before the game that I was going to play only one half. The TV commentators pointed out that I was standing on the sidelines with ice on my knee, but

**259**

they said that was strictly routine, strictly a precaution against swelling. It wasn't routine at all.

I really don't know whether I could have played the second half or not. I suppose I could have, with a shot of cortisone or something like that, but I don't know how the knee would have been afterward. (I was all right the following week, when we gave the New York Giants a proper introduction to the American Football League.)

My football career could end even before the 1969 American Football League season ends. I know that. I know that every day. I'm going to keep playing as long as I can play well, but as soon as I realize I'm not playing well, not passing the way I can, I'll quit. I've reached the point now where I just don't have any idea how long the knees are going to hold out. They could last one more game or one more season or five more seasons.

When my knees aren't strong enough for me to play my best or to play regularly, I'm not going to hang around just to pick up the pay check. I love football, but just as much as I love it, I think I'd hate standing on the sidelines.

I'd like to be around for the merger in 1970, when we get the Baltimore Colts and the Cleveland Browns and the Pittsburgh Steelers in the American Football League. I've been told that the Colts hope I'll be around for that, too, and I'd hate to disappoint them. I've heard they want to get even for the Super Bowl. Hell, there's no way they can get even. They can beat us ten times in a row, and it won't take away the fact that we beat them, and beat them good, when we were eighteen-point underdogs in Miami. I'll have that to remember the rest of my life. So will the Colts.

**260**

I'd like to be able to keep playing with the Jets because this is going to be a helluva football team for a long time. Our guys are young, most of them, and they're good, and they're going to get even better. I'd like to be part of that for a while.

But, shoot, I've got no complaints if my pro football career is over at the end of the 1969 football season. I'll have had five years of professional football, long enough to prove to myself that I could do the job. I don't care that much what other people think of my ability, as long as I know, and my teammates know.

I hope, and I think, that when I am finished with football, I'll be set up financially for the rest of my life. I don't need a lot of money to be happy. I've got Park Avenue tastes now, but I've got Beaver Falls tastes, too, and if I have to, I can adjust, I'm flexible.

If I'm lucky, and I've been lucky all my life, lucky in having a good family and good friends, maybe I'll have a career in the movie business. I'm pretty sure that'd be fun. The weather's nice in California, and so's the salary; the scenery's attractive, and so's the company.

Eventually, I know, I'm going to settle down and raise a family. I want to have kids; hell, I'm a kid myself in many ways. I hope I stay a kid for a long time. I hope I'll be able to laugh at silly things and laugh at serious things and never take myself too seriously. It's all right if other people want to take me seriously. But when I start taking myself seriously, I'll be in trouble. I know there's a bit of a wink behind everything I say and everything I do.

**261**

There are things I want to learn when I stop playing football. I want to learn foreign languages. I want to learn to play the guitar. I want to learn the kind of things that have nothing to do with playing football or making money.

The most important thing is that, no matter when I stop playing football, no matter what I do afterward, I'm going to have fun. I'm going to enjoy myself. All my life, I've enjoyed myself. I've enjoyed running with the gangs in Beaver Falls, and I've enjoyed roaming around a college town in an old beat-up car, and I've enjoyed leading the life of a professional football player, old enough to drink and old enough to chase and young enough to handle the two with pleasure. I really can't wait until tomorrow. It's going to be fun.

Want to bet on that?

**262**

# Life Is Never Dull
# with Joe Willie

BY DICK SCHAAP

The first time Joe Namath and I sat down to work on his autobiography, Joe began, with prompting, to tell a story about himself and a young lady, a story with a happy ending. "Can we use that in the book?" I said.

"Hell, yes," said Joe. "Anything I say, we can use in the book. Shoot, if I don't want something used, I won't say it."

For the next six months, there wasn't much that Joe Namath didn't say. He was open, he was candid and, best of all, he stood by what he said. He talked about all the things that athletes traditionally avoid—especially the three silent B's of the sports world, broads, booze and betting—and when he saw his words in cold type, he didn't flinch.

"That's the truth," he'd say, going over the manuscript. "That's the goldang truth."

When Joe and I first considered collaborating on his story, before we ever met, I wondered whether we could, together, arrive at the truth. Not knowing him, I feared that Joe, like other men who have been transformed in their own lifetimes to myths, might no longer recognize the truth; I feared he might believe his own mythology. And I feared, too, that even if Joe knew the truth, he might, again like other super-celebrities, have no desire to tell it. After all, he was in a position where he didn't have to tell the truth. People wanted to hear what Joe Namath had to say, whether he spoke the truth or not.

My worries were dispelled as soon as we met. Joe is almost compulsive about telling the truth, about hiding nothing. As he says in his autobiography, "I hardly ever lie. At least, I don't lie to guys." He won't even lie about lying. In the first draft of the book, I had quoted him as saying, "I don't lie," but he insisted upon modifying the phrase. "That's not true," he said. "I do lie sometimes, to girls."

Perhaps because he feels he has read so many lies about himself, Joe wanted his story to be accurate down to the tiniest detail. We argued for a long time over the exact composition of the brace he wears on his knee, whether it is made of rubber and steel or rubber and aluminum. The team doctor and the team trainer both said the brace was made of aluminium; Joe said it was steel. In the end, I went with Joe. He may be wrong, but he doesn't think so.

And he ought to know; he does come from a steel-mill town.

Joe worked on his autobiography; he didn't simply watch it take shape. He had to work hard to jog memories from his mind. Joe Namath is a "now" person; he doesn't live in the past at all. He has to force himself to recall details beyond the basic facts of his life. Joe is more interested in today than yesterday; he is also more interested in today than tomorrow.

We spent hundreds of hours together, playing golf (he won), drinking Scotch (he won) and, whenever possible, working with a tape recorder. We worked under a variety of conditions. Sometimes we recorded by the swimming pool at the Palm Bay Club in Miami, Joe's winter home, and on those tapes Joe's recollections alternate with his appropriate comments on the passing bikinis. Sometimes we recorded in Joe's apartment at the Palm Bay Club and sometimes in his apartment in New York, and on those tapes our dialogues have a musical background, the sounds of Bobbie Gentry or Aretha Franklin or The Fifth Dimension floating endlessly from a stereo system. Once we recorded for two straight hours on a plane from Miami to New York while Joe and I, thanks to his influence, shared a dozen small bottles of Scotch, well beyond the legal allotment of four. The stewardesses didn't break the rule, although they looked as though they might have been willing to do that, and more; instead, other passengers contributed their miniature bottles to the dozens of plaques, trophies and prizes gathered by Joe since the Super Bowl. Once, we recorded in the back seat of an open convertible,

267

cruising through the center of Beaver Falls, Pennsylvania, Joe's occasional comments cutting through a steady howl of greetings and cheers.

Joe was a thoroughly cooperative literary partner. He not only shared his memories and his opinions. He shared his life—up to a point, of course. Early in our relationship, he told me of the investigation of Bachelors III and warned me that it just might affect his story. I was with him the evening Pete Rozelle told him he might be suspended and I was with him the morning he announced his retirement. He took me along to his first private conference with Rozelle, and he phoned me from the commissioner's office the day he ended his retirement. "This is Joe," he said. "I've got something to tell you."

"What?"

"I've been suspended."

He was always needling. We had a ritual during the months of working together in Miami. I'd wake him each morning at nine thirty. "Good morning," he'd mumble.

"It's nine thirty."

"Go away."

"Want to work?"

"No."

"OK. See you tomorrow."

"I'll be down in twenty minutes."

After we had been working together for a few weeks, at the end of a day of recording, Joe turned to me and said, "You know, I can't wait until tomorrow."

"Why not?" I said, unsuspecting.

"Cause I get better-looking every day."

**268**

A few days later, I stumbled into the same trap. Again, Joe mentioned that he couldn't wait for the next day, and again I asked why, and again he told me. The line had to be the title for Joe's story. It is the essence of Joe Namath —the outrageously immodest line, the put-on, the sort of line that no one who is in his right mind could take seriously.

Of course, some people will take the line seriously and will condemn Joe as a braggart. He is not. He is a man with a sense of humor, a man who winks at life and winks at himself.

In his serious moments, which are extremely rare, Joe is the antithesis of the braggart. As he reviewed the manuscript of his autobiography, he deliberately edited out anything that smacked of serious immodesty, anything that sounded to him as though he were actually placing himself on a pedestal. In the Super Bowl section, for instance, Joe played down his own importance and insisted upon amplifying the text to give full credit to the Jet defense and the Jet blockers. He fought to minimize his own physical problems, to emphasize, instead, that everyone in professional football risked physical damage and that everyone, sooner or later, played in pain.

Joe removed from the manuscript incidents that he felt made him sound too good, almost saintly. He deleted a reference to the fact that the day after the Super Bowl, when Baltimore's Rick Volk was hospitalized with a concussion, he sent flowers to Volk, wishing him a speedy recovery. "That's got nothing to do with anything," Joe said. It did have something to do with everything, but

**269**

Joe wouldn't tell the story himself. I don't think he objects to my telling it; it's the truth. Joe just wouldn't say it himself.

Joe Namath is not an especially reflective man. He does not often second-guess himself—he hasn't had much reason to—or doubt his own motives. He believes in simplicity. There were two incidents, in particular, that I found more complex than Joe did and, each time, I tried to draw from him more information than actually existed. One incident was the Most Valuable Player voting among the New York Jets in 1967. Joe had come in sixth or seventh in the balloting—different accounts gave different results—and it seemed to me patently absurd that any first-string quarterback, even one less gifted and dominant than Joe, could be only the sixth or seventh most valuable player on his team. I knew that if I were Joe I would be deeply resentful of the voting; I expected him to be resentful, too, and I tried to prod him into expressing his resentment. There was only one problem. Joe wasn't resentful, and his rationale was so simple I refused at first to accept it. "I wasn't the most valuable player," he said. Period. That was it; that was Joe's complete reaction. Eventually, I realized that if Joe had any anger, it was directed only at himself for not playing better in 1967.

Similarly, we talked many times about Joe's decision to leave the Jets' training camp one night in 1967. "Personal problems," he said. I pressed him to be more specific, but Joe felt no need, or desire, to be more specific. "Too sentimental," he said. "Too much like feeling sorry for myself. I just had personal problems." Joe believed,

**270**

strongly, that personal problems were sufficient explanation for his act; he would have accepted that explanation from anyone else.

We didn't spend all our time working. We spent a lot of time laughing. I remember the day Joe was arrested in Miami and charged with reckless and drunken driving. We spent the entire day in his apartment, avoiding the photographers waiting by the entrance to the Palm Bay Club, and the phone rang all day long, Weeb Ewbank calling, Suzie Storm calling, Joe's mother calling, everybody worrying about Joe. "Don't worry," he told everyone. "Don't believe everything you read in the papers." He saw the absurdity of the situation. He had been speeding, but not dangerously (the drunken-driving charge was dropped). No one had been hurt; nothing had happened, except an argument with the arresting police officer. If the incident had involved almost anyone other than Joe Namath, it would never have made the papers. But because it was Joe, everyone got excited. Joe laughed and drank tequila Mexican style, alternately sucking on a lemon and licking salt off his wrist, and he and I and Mike Bite, his lawyer, putted for dollars on the living-room rug. Mike gave us both putting lessons; he also gave us both dollars.

Then there was a night in Bachelors III, when Joe sat me down next to a lady he knew, not an amateur, and she and I chatted about Joe. "He's got such a beautiful head," she said. "He's a beautiful conversationalist. He's got a sexy mouth. He's got the most beautiful blue eyes." (Later, when this remark was repeated to Joe, he blinked his green eyes and forgave her, saying, "Hell, she's never seen them

**271**

in the light.") The lady stared at Joe as he moved around the club, mixing with customers. The first time she met him, she recalled, she told Joe exactly, specifically, what she wanted to do with him that night. "He liked me right away," she said. "He knew I was for real."

Wherever Joe went, there was always exictement. When his friend Tom Jones opened at the Copacabana, Joe, through Bachelors III, took a table for forty, not at ringside but at the rear of the room. More than forty people showed up, so Joe, after making certain that his guests all had seats, stood through the show. The next night, he went to the Americana to hear The Fifth Dimension, and the show started late because the entire audience, mostly high school students celebrating their senior prom, stood and gave Joe an ovation that must have lasted five minutes. After the show, he visited with the members of The Fifth Dimension in their hotel suite, then brought them all back to Bachelors III for a celebration. Tom Jones showed up, and Paul Anka; and Joe, who had gone two days with no more than four hours of sleep, celebrated almost till dawn.

Through most of the crisis over Bachelors III, Joe managed to have fun. I remember sitting one day in the club with Joe and Jimmy Breslin, the writer, who was then running for the Democratic nomination for president of the New York City Council. Breslin wanted Joe's endorsement for himself and his running mate, Norman Mailer, and Joe, with no interest in politics, simply amused by Breslin, gave his endorsement. And then Breslin offered Namath advice in return. "Why don't you put a picture of

**272**

Capone in the window?" Breslin said, and Namath loved the idea.

They chatted about the Mafioso—both Breslin and Namath had heard that such an organization might exist—and they talked about tapped telephones. "There's so many taps on the phone in the men's room at the Copa," said Breslin, "the dime don't go down." Joe laughed.

The whole experience of collaborating with Joe Namath was pleasurable, pleasure mitigated only by the overriding uncertainty of whether or not Joe was going to play professional football in 1969. I didn't know the answer until the day Joe and Pete Rozelle jointly announced that they had reached an understanding. I don't think Joe knew the answer until then, either.

The night before, he sat in my apartment, with his lawyers, Mike Bite and Jimmy Walsh, and the four of us wondered exactly what was going to happen. We were laughing about our confusion, because so many people had approached each of us, thinking we knew the answer, and, at that moment, no more than sixteen hours before Joe and Rozelle made their peace, none of us could have given a confident prediction. My own guess changed from day to day—first I was pretty sure he would play; then I was pretty sure he wouldn't—reflecting Joe's fluctuating moods. I knew one thing for certain: The more the experts knowingly forecast that Joe would have to come back and play, the more they counseled him to give up his principle and accept his censure, then the more Joe leaned away from playing. Joe Namath does not like to be told what he should do; he also does not believe in telling other

**273**

people what they should do (except, of course, in the huddle).

Like most of the people around Joe, I respected him for his stand and, at the same time, hoped that he would play football. I was being selfish. Not for the book; I knew the book would stand up either way. But for my own pleasure, I wanted to watch Joe play football. There's no prettier spectacle, on the field or on television.

For Joe's sake, too, I'm glad he's playing football. I could see, all through the dispute over his ownership of Bachelors III, how much he wanted to play football. He would have spent a totally miserable, frustrating fall on the sidelines. The thing that Joe Namath does better than any other man in the world is pass a football. And I've got to go along with Joe's way of thinking: Everyone should do his own thing.

Before the Super Bowl game of 1969, I admit I was not one of the true believers. I thought the Baltimore Colts were going to destroy the New York Jets. I thought Joe Namath was going to be lucky to escape from the Orange Bowl with even one leg intact. And I thought, too, from what I'd read and what I'd heard, that Joe Namath was about as warm and likable as Ivan the Terrible.

I was wrong on all three counts.

I discovered how wrong I was on the first two very quickly—in two and a half hours on a Sunday afternoon, when the Jets and Joe impressively defeated the Baltimore Colts.

I discovered how wrong I was on the third during the

six months Joe and I worked on his autobiography. Working with Joe, as I've said, was fun. Getting to know Joe, trying to figure him out—trying to separate Joe Namath from the image of Joe Namath—was fascinating.

I'm not going to suggest that Joe Namath is a saint; he's not even in field-goal range. He has flaws. I've seen him rude, thoughtless, ill-tempered, impatient, overly sensitive to criticism. I've never spent hundreds of hours with anyone who didn't reveal faults.

But there are other aspects to Joe Namath that he cannot, or will not, discuss in his autobiography, aspects that are worth mentioning. Take his generosity. There are many athletes who pick up tabs and leave good tips—not as many as there are who don't, but, still, many. Most of the ones I've seen do it with a flourish, with trumpets—their own—blaring. Joe does it quietly. Almost no one ever gets a chance to pick up a tab if Joe is close to it; the bill is paid before anyone else knows it. He is a ridiculously lavish tipper, but he does that, too, without a show. He does not spend nearly so much money on clothes and entertaining himself as people suspect, but he hands his money away to cab drivers, doormen and waiters.

His loyalty to old friends is remarkable. His lawyers, Bite and Walsh, both go back to Alabama with him, and while he is in a position where he could hire a Louis Nizer or a Ted Sorenson if he wished, he sticks with the people he knows, the people he trusts. His loyalty is not limited to business dealings. There is, for example, a man named Dave Omograsso, from Beaver Falls, who works in New York City as a waiter. Omograsso is seven or eight years older than Joe, and they knew each other only slightly back home. But Omograsso came into Bachelors III one day and said hello to Joe, and Joe welcomed him and decided he was a helluva guy. "Hell, I like Dave," Joe says, "and Ray likes him, and we just like having him go around with us. If our positions were reversed, he'd do the same thing." Joe believes this about all his friends, that he is doing nothing more for them than they would do for him if they, rather than he, were on top. It is an innocent, but appealing, point of view.

I'm fairly sure that if Joe had his choice he would decree that all women in the world be beautiful and under the age of, say, twenty-five. Yet he seems to save his greatest charm for women over forty—he uses the Southern "Ma'am," and he uses it with respect—and the more a woman needs flattery, the more he gives it to her. He compliments the secretary in the steel-rimmed glasses more readily than he does the swinger in the micro-dress. "Aren't you pretty?" he'll say to a teenager who isn't, but who wants to be.

In our travels together, I didn't find one woman over forty who wasn't charmed by him. Of course, I didn't find too many under forty who weren't charmed, either. There were a few. Some seemed frightened, either by his style or by the thought of the competition involved. And during our Scotch-filled plane ride from Miami to New York I overheard one stewardess telling another, "Yes, he's nice, but I like that intellectual next to him better."

My record during our six months together was one win, 347 losses.

Joe has a genuine respect for his elders, for men as

well as women. He calls the men "sir" and he calls them "mister." Weeb Ewbank may be the only man in the world over fifty whom Joe calls by his first name.

Joe has, too, tremendous patience with autograph seekers. If he is not in a hurry, if he is, say, walking along the streets of Manhattan, with no special destination, he will not simply sign an autograph and slip away.

Once, on First Avenue, a boy in his teens came sprinting up to us from across the street, out of breath more from excitement than exercise. He asked for Joe's signature. "I play football, too," the boy said. "I never thought I'd see you. I never thought I'd meet you."

Joe smiled, one of his strongest weapons. "What's your name?" he said.

"Ron."

"To Ron," Joe wrote, "with best wishes from all the New York Jets. Joe Willie Namath." (To young girls, Joe usually writes, "Stay sweet." During the period of his retirement, he dropped the "from all the New York Jets" phrase from his autographs. "Sure saves a lot of time," he said.)

"What position do you play?"

"Center," the boy said.

Joe patted him on the back and wished him luck, and the boy raced away.

A block farther north, a middle-aged man asked if he could have Joe's autograph for his son. "I'm sorry to bother you," the man said. "I know you must hate this."

"It's all right," Joe said. "What's your boy's name?"

Joe Namath may be the only man in New York City

who actually seems to know most of his neighbors. He has created his own small town in the middle of Manhattan. When he walks out of his apartment building on the corner of First Avenue and 76th Street, a man across the street hollers hello from his terrace. Joe responds with a personal greeting. He knows the owner of the dry-cleaning store, the guy sweeping up in front of the bar, the cashier in the luncheonette.

He is, genuinely, a friendly person. He likes people and, for the most part, he trusts them. Once, when we were sitting at breakfast in the Palm Bay Club, Joe received a collect telephone call from a man in a small town in Alabama. On a whim, although he didn't recognize the man's name, Joe accepted the call. The man wanted to know if Joe would send him $150 to place a tombstone by the graves of his mother and father. The man sounded sincere to Joe, and Joe sent him the $150. Joe said that someday he thought he'd like to stop up and see the man and visit the cemetery.

During the period when Joe was temporarily retired, a young man came to the door of his Manhattan apartment and said that he was trying to win a contest selling magazine subscriptions. He suggested that Joe, instead of buying the magazines for himself, order them and have them sent to patients in veterans' hospitals. Joe said he'd take $223 worth of magazine subscriptions.

The night that Joe went to the Tom Jones opening, just as he was about to leave Bachelors III, a very plain-looking girl walked up to him and explained that she and her friends all worked in the same office and that they had

**278**

come to Bachelors III to catch a glimpse of Joe Namath. "Would you have a drink with us?" she said.

Joe sat down with the girls from the office for thirty minutes. His friends waited for him at the Copa.

Ultimately, Joe's greatest strength is his insistence upon being honest about himself, upon presenting himself to the public the way he is in private. If anything, he leans over backward, hiding his strengths more than his weaknesses.

Yet there are thousands of people, perhaps even hundreds of thousands, who feel, sincerely, that Joe Namath is a bad example to the young people of America. They want their sports heroes to be by Jack Armstrong out of Frank Merriwell—nonsmoking, nondrinking, nonwomanizing. They conveniently forget that the greatest American athlete of the twentieth century—Jim Thorpe—and the greatest American professional athlete of the twentieth century—Babe Ruth—would have looked upon Joe's actions with nothing worse than envy.

There are race riots in every major city in the United States. There is a senseless war going on in Vietnam. There are people starving in sections of the most affluent country in the history of the world. And, still, some people are afraid that the youth of America will turn out bad because Joe Namath admits he enjoys Scotch, girls and gambling. Those people could learn a lot from Joe—about honesty, about perspective—a lot more than simply how to throw a football.

ABOUT THE AUTHORS

**Joseph William Namath** was born in Beaver Falls, Pennsylvania, on May 31, 1943. He is a quarterback and a bachelor, not necessarily in that order. He attended the University of Alabama, joined the New York Jets in 1965 and was named the Most Valuable Player in the 1969 Super Bowl game. He won the 1969 Hickok Belt award as the outstanding professional athlete in the United States. He used to be in the restaurant business in New York City.

**Dick Schaap** was born in Brooklyn, New York, on September 27, 1934. He is neither a quarterback nor a bachelor. A graduate of Cornell University and the Columbia School of Journalism, he has been sports editor and senior editor of *Newsweek,* city editor of the *New York Herald Tribune* and a syndicated columnist. He collaborated with Jerry Kramer of the Green Bay Packers on *Instant Replay* and *Jerry Kramer's Farewell to Football.* His other books include *R. F. K., Turned On* and *An Illustrated History of the Olympics.*